SECRET
PITTSBURGH

A Guide to the Weird, Wonderful, and Obscure

Karyn Locke

Reedy Press
PO Box 5131
St. Louis, MO 63139
www.reedypress.com

Library of Congress Control Number: 2020938248
ISBN: 9781681062846

Design by Jill Halpin

Printed in the United States of America
20 21 22 23 24   5 4 3 2 1

To Mr. Locke for being Pittsburgh's #1 fan and the most supportive husband in the universe. I mean, I have to assume there are husbands on undiscovered planets, right?

To Molly for being the coolest "kid" and shoulder to bounce ideas off of. Happy graduation, even though you had to have a virtual one.

To GrandPam for her selflessness, unwavering support, and home-baked goodies.

And to the city of Pittsburgh for being 93% inspiration, 6% historic-cool, 4% beautiful, and 2% fudge ripple.

Thank you.

CONTENTS

ACKNOWLEDGMENTS

Although there were times during the writing of this book when I felt like Don Music, the piano player with writer's block from *Sesame Street*, really digging into the city of Pittsburgh, both past and present, was a pleasure. And without the following folks, this book wouldn't have been nearly as fun to write:

First, a Pittsburgh-Penguins-Stanley-Cup-Parade-sized thank you to Mr. Locke for his photographic eye and gorgeous images printed throughout the book. Also, not once did I hear, "How are you planning to fit a book into an already-packed day?" but instead received all the positive affirmation a girl could ever want.

A giant-Pittsburgh-parking-chair thank you to Visit Pittsburgh for helping with information and being downright gracious to the girl across the border in Ohio, especially Tom Loftus and Kristin Wenger.

To Reedy Press, thank you for taking a chance on a first-time book writer.

To my college Creative Writing Class professor: thank you for allowing me to realize that it's okay to not write like everybody else.

Thank you to Pittsburgh Cultural Trust for letting me delve into the Pittsburgh art scene so seamlessly.

INTRODUCTION

When starting to compile the people and places mentioned in this book, it was a happy labor of love. While it often included a "one step forward, two more steps forward" way of writing—compliments of finding more cool items to add with every item researched—I learned so much more about my big city, Pittsburgh, than I'd ever thought possible and refuse to call that a problem.

And it was delving into Pittsburgh's history, locations, and culture that made me fall in love with it more than I already had. Bones of Saints inside a catholic church? We've got them. A unique bridge paint color with a portmanteau name? We've got that too. And what about meals fit for a US president, a unique dialect, or transportation colors that inspired Fred Rogers's set pieces? Check.

So, not only do we have one of the most gorgeous skylines in the world, we've got the best "front door view" to boot. *Secret Pittsburgh* was written for Pittsburgh visitors, its locals, and for folks that love a good backstory on locations around the city.

STEEPED IN DANGER

Why does San Francisco get the claim to fame for steep streets when Pittsburgh has the steepest street in the United States?

If you've always thought that San Francisco had the steepest street in America compliments of all the city's publicity, fun tales of folks challenging their skills by maneuvering down its zigzagging roads, and all the photos of either top or bottom views throughout the years, you may be pleasantly surprised to learn that Pittsburgh gets to claim the steepness title. While the entire street comes in at a not-so-long 630 feet, Canton Avenue in the Beechview area of town gets the official honor due to its lower-end portion.

With a whopping 37 percent incline stretching only 21 feet in length, signs noting the accolade are posted at both ends to deter drivers from going up or down (or sideways), but that hasn't stopped folks from testing both their luck and driving skills, especially in winter, because it technically is a drivable street.

The avenue is not paved but instead is covered in cobblestones, making the trek a bumpy one should you be up for the challenge. For those who want a cycling thrill, Pittsburgh has an annual Dirty Dozen bike race that tests its participants' abilities by racing over the 13 steepest streets in the city at top speed via two wheels—Canton Avenue being one of them.

Don't try to drive up or down the steepest part of Canton Avenue—a walk will be safer.

This is the
STEEPEST STREET
in the Continental United States.

Pittsburgh is famous for its steel-producing heritage; it's *infamous* for its hills.

Beechview is not for the faint of heart, but that's part of its charm. You don't just stroll through this neighborhood. You have to conquer it.

Canton Avenue is the steepest street in the Continental United States at an ankle-straining 37% grade, but it's not alone. Once you've climbed this hill, try these other Beechview challenges: Boustead Ave (29%), Hampshire Avenue (23%), Fallowfield Avenue (22%), Belasco Avenue (21%), and Dagmar Avenue(20%).

It's official! Pittsburgh has the steepest street in the continental United States!
Photo credit: Steven Locke

STEEPEST STREET IN AMERICA

WHAT Canton Avenue

WHERE 1601 Canton Ave.

COST Free

PRO TIP Canton Avenue is treacherous even on the best of days so visiting when it's clear and without snow or ice is best.

1 + 1 = 1?

How does the combination of two major Pennsylvania rivers make a very well-known US river?

At the tip of the Golden Triangle area of downtown Pittsburgh sits a particularly special place: it's the spot where two prominent Pittsburgh rivers join together to make a completely new waterway, the Ohio River, that meanders between Pennsylvania and Ohio and eventually makes its way to the mighty Mississippi. While Point State Park is not only a gorgeous spot to enjoy picnics and outdoor recreation (think biking, running, and boating), head down near the water's edge by its popular fountain, and you can stand on the brass marker that signifies the exact spot where the rivers meet.

The 325-mile-long Allegheny River gets its start in Potter County, Pennsylvania, and then meanders its way into New York and back into Pennsylvania to meet up with the Monongahela River, a 127-mile-long waterway beginning in Fairmont, West Virginia. It's this confluence that creates the famous 981-mile-long Ohio River that takes a turn west to eventually end up meeting the Mississippi River in Illinois.

And don't think Pittsburgh doesn't know how good it is to have this cool feature. There are plenty of tributes to it: The Three Rivers Arts Festival in summer and the Three Rivers Heritage Trail are just a couple of well-known references to this confluence.

TWO PITTSBURGH RIVERS FORMING INTO ONE

WHAT Confluence of Pittsburgh's three rivers

WHERE Point State Park, 601 Commonwealth Pl.

COST Free

PRO TIP Visiting any time of year is lovely, but a visit during spring, summer, or fall makes for some very pretty photos.

One river plus one river does equal three rivers when it comes to the Ohio River and Pittsburgh's Golden Triangle. Photo credit: Steven Locke

Pittsburgh rivers average 16–17 feet in depth. If they rise above 18 feet, parking at Mon Wharf parking lot in downtown is flooded.

ALLOHMON OR AZTEC GOLD?

Why does Pittsburgh's bridge paint get a special name?

Considering that the three rivers in Pittsburgh are such a prominent feature of the city, it would only make sense to mention the bridges that span across them. If you've ever driven, biked, ran, jogged, or even taken a leisurely walk across a few of the bridges in downtown Pittsburgh, it's impossible not to notice the special color that ties in to Pittsburgh's official city colors: bright yellow. Technically, the color is called Aztec Gold. So, why the reference to the fifth-century Mesoamerican culture in Central Mexico?

In a nutshell, the downtown Pittsburgh area has been dubbed the Golden Triangle due to its scenic beauty and the way it starts in a peak at Point State Park and forms a triangle shape compliments of its rivers' positions on either side. So, taking a cue from the fun nickname, Aztec Gold certainly fits.

Locals have given the color another name, AllOhMon. It's a combination of the first syllables of all three rivers flowing into the Golden Triangle. So, no matter what name you give the downtown bridge color, you certainly won't forget the view each bridge provides.

ALLOHMON BRIDGE PAINT

WHAT Pittsburgh bridges

WHERE All over the city

COST Free

PRO TIP As with many Pittsburgh bridges, you're free to walk, drive, or bike over them, but the Sister Bridges connecting the North Shore to downtown are really worth moseying across for the gorgeous views of the Allegheny River.

The Three Sisters Bridges in downtown Pittsburgh not only share the Aztec Gold color but are identical in shape as well.

It's not yellow, it's the color AllOhMon on downtown Pittsburgh bridges.
Photo credit: Steven Locke

THE MOST HEAVILY PAINTED OBJECT IN THE WORLD

How does a barrier between two old colleges make for the most frequently painted object in the world?

Once just an object to separate two college campus sections, the Fence at Carnegie Mellon University in Oakland became a billboard and bonding spot for its students. Originally a wooden fence built in 1923 in "the Cut," an area that separated Carnegie Tech from Margaret Morrison Women's School, the students' use of it evolved and the fence became a billboard to promote school events, meet and hang out with other students, show general support for sororities and fraternities, and to highlight sports teams.

Sadly, the original wooden fence stood for only 70 years and collapsed due to its own weight in 1993—six inches of paint thick! These days, the Fence is now made of much more durable concrete with reinforced steel, but the rules of its predecessor are still carried on: it may only be painted between midnight and dawn, and two

Between 1993 and 2007, 609 coats of paint were applied to the Fence.

The Fence at Carnegie Mellon University is well on its way to becoming the most painted object in the world—again! Photo credit: Steven Locke

representatives of the latest paint job must stand duty during painting hours or risk their artistic creation being taken over by another team. And, if guards weren't enough, painters really get into the school spirit by having barbecuing parties during their time on duty!

Before the wooden version of the Fence collapsed, the *Guinness Book of World Records* called it "The World's Most Painted Object." These days, CMU students are adding paint layer by layer to try to win back the title.

HOUDINI JUMPED THE BRIDGE

Why did one of the most famous magicians in the world jump from a Pittsburgh bridge?

On May 22, 1907, Hungarian-born Vaudeville magician Harry Houdini made his way to a prominent Pittsburgh River to perform one of his jaw-dropping stunts: while tied to a rope and donning handcuffs, he plunged into the freezing cold water of the Allegheny River and escaped while submerged. Another successful attempt the next year on March 13, 1908 (and in much colder water), gave him an uneasy feeling due to his superstitious nature for the number 13.

However, a few years later in 1916, 42-year old Houdini would stun the crowd (and promote his new show) at the Davis Theater by being hung upside down in a straitjacket and escaping his precarious situation in plain view. Delighting the onlookers, his stunt on the corner of Liberty Avenue and Wood Street is one that not only showcased his ability to get out of a tight situation but also proved him to be a true showman.

As a tribute to Houdini's visits to the city and his magical stunts, Pittsburgh Cultural Trust recreates the promotion in the front window of its intimate show venue, Liberty Magic, with a life-sized display. Highlighting a single magician at a time, this stunt not only offer viewers a look at how magic has evolved, but the intimate setting in a speakeasy style also delights audiences who enjoy up-close magic.

Harry Houdini's most famous trick was the Chinese Water Torture Cell.

The life-sized tribute to Harry Houdini in the front window of Liberty Magic. Photo credit: Steven Locke

HARRY HOUDINI'S ESCAPE ATTEMPTS

WHAT Liberty Magic featuring Harry Houdini's magic stunt

WHERE 811 Liberty Ave.

COST During open hours, the tribute is in the lobby and is free to view

PRO TIP Check for times for Liberty Magic so you can go inside and view.

www.trustarts.org

EMOTICON-ING OUR FEELINGS

How does one of the most-used Internet icons get its claim to fame from Pittsburgh?

If you've been anywhere near a computer and a keyboard in the past four decades and have had a pleasant conversation with someone else on it or even just a few quick words, you've undoubtedly seen the smiley emoticon used to portray the true meaning of what another is writing: a colon, dash, and closed parenthesis typed in succession to form a sideways smiley face, nose included.

But, did you know that a professor from Carnegie Mellon University invented the typed icon? On September 19, 1982, Scott Fahlman from the Computer Science department of CMU created the smile emoticon during the time when email was very new and messages were sent without pictures, using only the English language.

Just as online bulletin boards were in their infancy, Fahlman made up the three-character emoticon to mitigate potentially misconstrued messages, and it really took off. In addition to the happy face, he created a similar combination of characters but with an open parenthesis to convey sadness and anger. In only a

---

FIRST EMOTICON

WHAT The smiley emoticon

WHERE All over the Internet

COST Only the effort to press the colon, dash, and closed parenthesis keys on your computer

PRO TIP Smiley emoticons make the Internet world a better place, so use them liberally.

As of March 2020, there were more than 3,400 emojis in the Unicode Standard.

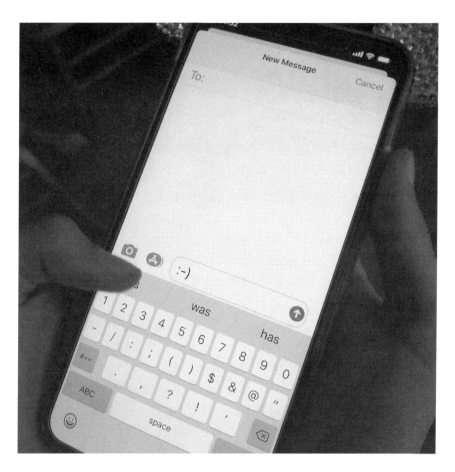

A colon, a dash, and closed parenthesis = one well-used emoticon.
Photo credit: Karyn Locke

few months' time, variations of the happy characters were all over computer network message boards. While we still use the three-character emoticon, computers and smartphones automatically turn it into an actual smiley face, along with hundreds of other emojis that convey even more emotions.

WOOD YOU CARE TO DRIVE?

Why does one of the shortest streets in Pittsburgh not have blacktop as its surface?

If the one-way, nonlinear Pittsburgh streets weren't enough to pique one's driving and navigating curiosity, consider Roslyn Place in the Shadyside area of Pittsburgh. At only 250 feet in length, the entire road is paved with small wooden blocks, making it look like Pittsburgh roads from the early 20th century.

Once part of Aiken Farms, Thomas Rodd purchased the land where Roslyn Place now sits and turned it into large estates with pretty views. To ease both travel to and from the estates for owners and their guests, a mere five men took on the task of building the road and, after taking six months to cut the 26,000 wooden blocks, Roslyn Place became an official Pittsburgh street in 1914.

While the street may be small, it sure does pack a punch: 18 side-by-side-by-side homes line the road and it's the last of its kind in the city, not to mention one of only a handful left in the world. The street is very narrow (with vehicles parked on either side of it, there's barely room for a single driving lane. So, if you do feel like driving down it, be prepared to back up to leave) but the almost fairytale-like ambiance makes you feel like you've left the city and stepped foot into a children's book.

Homeowners on Roslyn Place have been known to keep wooden blocks to make their own street repairs.

An up-close look at the wood pavers lining Rosyln Place in Shadyside. Photo credit: Steven Locke

STREET MADE COMPLETELY OF WOOD

WHAT Roslyn Place wooden street

WHERE Roslyn Place

COST Free to walk, view, or drive on

PRO TIP Visit Roslyn Place on good-weather days so you can really see the grain of the wood lining the street.

An official designated historic landmark, Roslyn Place has survived over a century of wear and tear, buggies, and vehicles, and many street residents keep replacement wooden blocks left over from its massive restoration in 1985 to help with the upkeep. Today, only minor repairs need to be made on the old-school street.

WHERE THE STREETS HAVE NO PAVE

When are streets in Pittsburgh not streets at all?

If you've ever heard of the term paper street, it's a title given to designate a road that appears on an official city map but has never technically been built. Called paper streets because they technically only exist on paper, many times city planners had very good intentions of making proper, drivable roads but they never came to fruition for a multitude of reasons. But, in the case of Pittsburgh, several of these paper roads became steep, public stairways instead of leaving the land as is.

To add to the head-scratching curiosity, Pittsburgh, along with many other hilly cities in the United States, considers its public staircases official city streets. And in the case of the South Side Slopes, several of its paper-street staircases have even been given official street names.

Don't think of these steep-step streets as your average staircase, either: Josephine Street has 284 total steps with Eleanor Street coming in close behind at 282—that's a rigorous leg (and cardiovascular system) workout for sure, but well worth the effort.

"STREET"LESS STREET NAMES

WHAT South Side Slopes "Streets"

WHERE South Side Pittsburgh

COST Free

PRO TIP Wear sturdy shoes— there are plenty of steps to climb up and down.

www.southsideslopes.org

An average mile is about 2,000 steps, making the 2,500 total stairs well over a mile long if put end to end.

Steps named after streets on the South Side? Yep! Photo credit: Steven Locke

Originally built to give workers living in the Slopes a means to get to work in The Flats area of the city below, the steps have now become a modern way for folks to see the gorgeous skyline.

With roughly 2,500 steps in the neighborhood, there's no reason for not taking advantage of the fun step route with an official walking tour. With 379 steps up and 441 steps down, the Church Route highlights the unique stairways, along with playgrounds, Pittsburgh architecture, and, of course, churches.

DON'T RUN OVER MY CHAIR!

How does a summer backyard staple make for an ideal space saver?

In Pittsburgh, with its steep, narrow streets and side-by-side houses in many popular neighborhoods, an unusual way to save a parking space has become a way of life for Steel City residents: the parking chair. Due to the increase in the number of vehicles needing to be parked in front of residents' homes, the harsh and snowy winter weather, and the desire to keep the place where you've just invested all of your shoveling effort open, the iconic parking chair is used to save the spot in a freshly shoveled-out area or to keep people from parking in front of a driveway running perpendicular to a roadway.

Generally, the Pittsburgh parking chair is plastic to endure the four-season Pittsburgh climate, but you'll see everything from '80s lawn chairs to dining-room-table-chairs—all used to hold residents' parking spots.

So, when did the parking chair become an official tradition? No one's truly certain but the hoopla surrounding the habit started in the 1990s when it became Pittsburgh parking nostalgia.

If you're wondering if the act is legal or not, well, technically there's no law in Pittsburgh stating that it's illegal to do so. However, city workers and officials don't

---

The tourist information center, Visit Pittsburgh, has a giant eight-foot parking chair that is moved to different locations around the city and is ideal for photos. Check its website for times and locations.

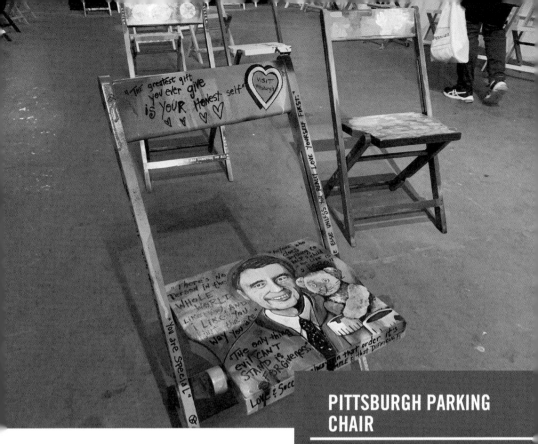

A Fred Rogers parking chair tribute.
Photo credit: Steven Locke

seem to object to its residents
using chairs for this purpose
unless it's a deterring object
(like blocking someone else's
driveway) or impeding traffic.

PITTSBURGH PARKING CHAIR

WHAT A Unique way to save your parking spot

WHERE Streets across the city

COST Free to view, but you can purchase your own

PRO TIP The iconic chair is more prominent in winter, so keep an eye out.

I'M INCLINED TO GO TO WORK

How does a clever means of traversing the Pittsburgh hills from the 1800s still make for a fun ride today?

If you're into fancy words, the technical term for a Pittsburgh incline is a funicular railway. And while that term may impress your friends, we like to simply call them inclines. Created in the 19th century as an easier means for workers to get up and down steep Pittsburgh hills, some even were used to move large working animals as well.

At one time, Pittsburgh had well over 20 inclines all across the city as a means of transportation, but only two have survived and are still in operation today: the Duquesne Incline and the Monongahela Incline.

The Duquesne Incline is undoubtedly the more prominent of the two with its two bright red and yellow cars. And, if you'd like a little Pittsburgh trivia to tie in with it, Fred Rogers used the same vivid hues to make the Neighborhood Trolley. Connecting Mt. Washington to Station Square, it runs daily, even on holidays, and costs five dollars for a round-trip fare. If you like behind-the-scenes tours, the incline offers a self-guided one where you can actually see the turning, working wheels that allow the set of inclines to run smoothly.

The Monongahela Incline offers a more understated exterior but serves the same basic route from Mt. Washington to Station

---

FUNICULAR RAILWAYS OF PITTSBURGH

WHAT Pittsburgh inclines

WHERE Station Square and Mt. Washington

COST $5 per round trip

PRO TIP Take either incline at least once during the day and at night for different, but still gorgeous, views of the skyline.

www.duquesneincline.org

Bright red and yellow are not only the colors of the Duquesne Incline, they're the same as the trolley in Mister Rogers' Neighborhood. Photo credit: Steven Locke

Square. Similar in trip cost, the choice between the two all depends on where you need to be or where you've parked.

Once you're moving, the ride is less than five minutes each way.

A SILENT NIGHT—INTERRUPTED BY RADIO

How did the interruption of Morse code become the first voice radio broadcast?

Up until the year 1906, all that was ever heard over wireless operators' earphones were the droning dots and dashes of Morse code, but everything changed on Christmas Eve of that year. A group of operators listening to the usual short and long beeps were suddenly startled by the interruption of a man's voice telling the story of Jesus's birth from the Gospel of Luke.

Afterwards, they heard "Silent Night," making it the first song to ever be played across a radio signal. A quick "Merry Christmas" wish was sent to all who were listening, and back to Morse code it went.

The man behind the first voice radio broadcast was Reginald Fessenden. But it wasn't until 1907 that Lee de Forest created a radio tube that was practical and effective to use for vocals. Thirteen years later, the radio really became a home staple when Westinghouse improved upon the idea and offered programming, getting Dr. Frank Conrad (a local ham-radio broadcaster) to start an official program in the city.

The official date of the first commercial broadcast was November 2, 1920, by station KDKA. Pittsburghers still listen (and watch) the station for local information and news.

While KDKA television is in downtown Pittsburgh near Point State Park, KDKA Radio is in Green Tree.

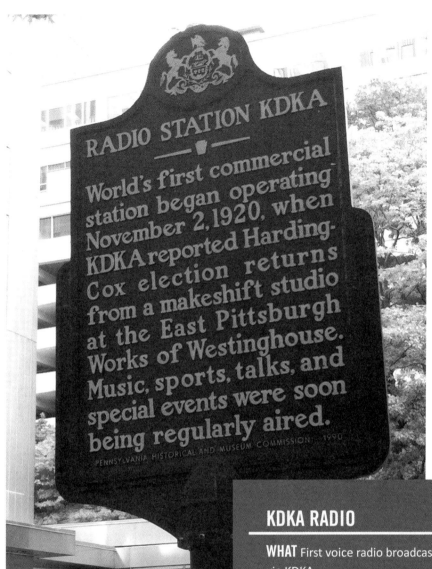

A sign highlighting the first KDKA Radio broadcast. Photo credit: www.flickr.com/photos/84408888@N00/

KDKA RADIO

WHAT First voice radio broadcast via KDKA

WHERE Foster Plaza 5, 651 Holiday Dr. Suite 300

COST Free to walk around the building

PRO TIP KDKA is still a prominent station in Pittsburgh, so feel free to listen in daily.

kdkaradio.radio.com

WHEELS IN HIS HEAD

How did a child's play toy become a beloved fair ride?

As a child, George Washington Gale Ferris Jr., loved a good water wheel to play with. So, it's absolutely no surprise that he turned his fascination with how things work into an engineering degree in 1880. Turning that love into money, he established G.W.G Ferris and Company in Pittsburgh and began a career as a local industrial site inspection engineer.

Then, in 1890, a challenge was issued at a banquet in Chicago that Ferris attended. Engineers were invited to design a giant structure for the Columbian Exposition coming in 1893 that would make the famous Eiffel Tower in Paris pale in comparison. Days after the challenge was made, Ferris crafted the plans for a giant "Ezekiel's Wheel" on a dining napkin and showed it to other engineers who immediately balked at the idea. But that didn't stop Ferris.

Using $25,000 of his own money, intricate blueprints were drafted and shown to the exposition's directors. One of them commented, "He has wheels in his head." But Ferris won over some of the directors, and the go-ahead was given, but only if he built it with his own money.

The 250-foot-diameter wheel made its first rotation on June 21, 1892, to the delight of riders who paid 50 cents for a 20-minute spin.

Present day, the largest Ferris wheel in the world is in the United States. Coming in at a whopping 550-feet in height, the

FERRIS WHEEL

WHAT George Ferris Jr.'s whimsical impact on amusement Park rides

WHERE Historical marker location located at West Commons at Arch Street near S. Diamond Street

COST Free to view the marker

PRO TIP Think of Mr. Ferris the next time you're stopped at the top of a Ferris wheel.

A Ferris wheel, no matter where it's located, can bring back beautiful memories. Photo credit: Steven Locke

High Roller in Las Vegas, Nevada, beat the previous record of the 541-foot tall Singapore Flyer by 9 feet. Opened in 2014, each of its 28 open-air cabins allows for up to 40 passengers each and has eight flat screen televisions to watch during the 30-minute ride.

The largest Ferris wheel in the world at 550 feet tall, the High Roller can be found on the Las Vegas Strip.

YOU WANT A MAP WITH THAT?

How did a popular vehicle become the inspiration for the first gas station?

By 1913, the Ford Motor Company had Model Ts coming off the line every three minutes. That amount of efficiency gave Gulf Refining Company the idea to create a pagoda-shaped service station on the corner of Baum Boulevard and St. Clair Street in Pittsburgh to keep up with gasoline demand. With its large sign labeled "GOOD GULF GASOLINE", drivers could drive up, get gas and service, and then drive all the way around the station in a circle to exit.

On opening day (a Tuesday), 30 gallons of gasoline were sold. By the following Saturday, sales were well over 350 gallons, all sold for 27 cents each. To put prices into perspective, if we take good old inflation into account, 27 cents a gallon in 1913 would equal about seven dollars today.

The station offered not only gas, but oils and lubricants as well. And if that weren't enough full-service attention, drivers could also get their tires replaced or filled with air, free water, and, of course, road maps to help them get where they needed to be.

GULF GAS STATION

WHAT First gas station location

WHERE Corner of Baum Boulevard and St. Clair Street

COST The gas station is no longer there but you can visit the original location.

PRO TIP Be thankful that you no longer need to try to read a road map thanks to Google Maps!

The cost of a brand new 1913 Ford Model T just off the assembly line was $525.

Gulf Refining Co. started a trend—the gas station! Photo credit: www.flickr.com/photos/ gerrydincher/

In December of the same year, and five miles away from the city proper, Gulf Refining Company became such a huge hit that thousands of service stations were opened across the country by different companies. And while gas stations are more of a literal stop-and-go-style these days—they certainly make for convenience—80 percent of convenient stores still offer gasoline to their customers.

PLAY BALL!

Why is Pittsburgh known for its baseball stadiums?

Up until 1909, if you wanted to catch the Pittsburgh Pirates playing a game of baseball, you'd have to park yourself on an uncomfortable wooden seat at the small Exposition Park. But everything changed that year for baseball fans (and Pittsburghers) with the opening of Forbes Field, named after the French and Indian War hero, John Forbes.

Pittsburgh businessman, Barney Dreyfus, collaborated with local steel tycoon, Andrew Carnegie, to build the massive ballpark in Oakland, and, to the delight of Pirates fans on June 30, 1909, the stadium opened to admit the 30,388 avid devotees who watched the first game in the brand-new park.

But why was it so special? It offered elevators to upper levels, luxury suites, and a three-tiered grandstand. Sadly, on June 28, 1970, showing its age and in need of extensive updates, beloved Forbes Field hosted its final Pirates game, making way for Three Rivers Stadium, which no longer stands either. In its heyday, Forbes Field hosted four World Series and two All-Star Games.

These days, PNC Park on the North Shore keeps baseball lovers happy. ESPN.com even dubbed the field "The Best Stadium in Major League Baseball" when it opened in 2001! With the ability to host 38,362 baseball fans, it has 96,750 square feet of Kentucky bluegrass on its playing surface.

WHY IS PITTSBURGH KNOWN FOR ITS BASEBALL STADIUMS?

WHAT Pittsburgh baseball stadiums

WHERE Forbes Field no longer exists, but you can visit the original home plate at University of Pittsburgh's Hillman Hall where it's only 15 feet from the original location.

COST Free

PRO TIP Make sure to check visiting hours before you go.

www.ballparksofbaseball.com

Gorgeous view of the Sister Bridges from the upper level at PNC Park. Photo credit: Steven Locke

With the cost of $262 million to build, its upper levels offer beautiful views of the Pittsburgh skyline and the three famous Sister Bridges. And if you really like fun Pittsburgh stadium facts, it's only 443 feet, 4 inches to the Allegheny River from home plate.

Andrew Carnegie was not only a stern businessman but also an investor and philanthropist.

LET'S HAVE SOME MAKE-BELIEVE

How does a beloved children's TV show still make us remember public television so fondly?

If you grew up in the latter half of the 20th century, and especially if you were from Pittsburgh, you knew of (and undoubtedly watched) the public television children's show, *Mister Rogers' Neighborhood*. You probably also knew that as soon as its famous red-and-yellow trolley made an appearance, it was time for some fun in the Neighborhood of Make-Believe.

But, have you ever wondered how the set pieces would look up close and whatever happened to them all after Fred Rogers retired? Happily, you don't have to dig around to find some of the show's most prominent and iconic props.

At Heinz History Center on the fourth floor, there's a large, dedicated space for Henrietta Pussycat and X the Owl's two-door Great Oak Tree, King Friday XIII's light blue castle, and even Chef Brockett's hat and apron.

But the nostalgia doesn't end there. The Center has a facsimile of the front room in Mister Rogers's cottage-style house where he religiously took off (and put back on) his house shoes (a.k.a. blue Sperrys), including a life-size figure of our hero himself—complete with Picture Picture (a type of slide projector).

If you're a true fan of the Neighborhood of Make-Believe, head to Children's Museum Pittsburgh and check out the original

---

Until finding their new place at Heinz History Center, both castle and tree set pieces were at WQED Pittsburgh in Oakland.

Both the tree and castle from Mister Rogers' Neighborhood *can be viewed at Heinz History Center. Photo credit: Steven Locke*

puppets from the Neighborhood of Make-Believe as well. In addition to the well-worn hand puppets that Fred Rogers voiced himself, you can spy an original sweater from the show. Hand-knitted by his mother (all of his sweaters were), it's found along with poignant photos of Rogers and a piano to try your hands at a popular show tune that we all sang along to.

NEIGHBORHOOD OF MAKE BELIEVE AT HEINZ HISTORY CENTER

WHAT *Mister Rogers' Neighborhood* set pieces

WHERE 1212 Smallman St.

COST Adults $18, Senior Citizens (62+) $15, Children 6-17 and Students with ID $9, Children under age 5 free.

PRO TIP While you'll definitely want to visit the memorabilia, make sure to carve out a couple of extra hours to see the Center in its entirety for a walk down Pittsburgh memory lane.

www.heinzhistorycenter.org

COME ON IN, THE DOOR'S OPEN

When can you get a behind-the-scenes peek at prominent Pittsburgh buildings?

A curious nature for what exists behind the scenes in old buildings may get you into trouble if you check them out without permission, but that's definitely not true during the autumn season for Pittsburgh architecture lovers and fans of cool building facts. Each October, and for one weekend only, dozens of buildings around the downtown area and in Oakland (new for this year) open their doors to let folks get a peek at architectural features they're not normally privy to. The annual event is officially called Doors Open Pittsburgh, and it continues to get bigger and better with each season that passes.

During this event, guests are able to explore spaces they've never seen before or go behind the scenes to check out what they've only dreamt of in their imaginations. But the fun doesn't end there, happily. Live storytellers are on-site to give scope to what makes each of

DOORS OPEN PITTSBURGH

WHAT A weekend of behind-the-scenes peeks at prominent Pittsburgh buildings.

WHERE Locations around Pittsburgh

COST Free

PRO TIP If you really want to learn about unseen locations, make sure to visit the website ahead of time and come up with a walking/driving plan so you're not zigzagging around the city.

www.doorsopenpgh.org

The event is self-paced, so you can be as ambitious or as laid-back as you'd like.

One of the Dollar Bank lions on display after its restoration, viewable during Doors Open Pittsburgh. Photo credit: Steven Locke

the 50-60 buildings unique to Pittsburgh. Past highlights have included checking out the working mechanics of a bank vault and even ringing the bell in a church belfry.

If you want to know something truly astounding about the event, it's this: there's only one person officially on the staff to make the event run smoothly. The rest are volunteers, happy to give their time to curious visitors.

STOP DOWNTOWN, GET A FREE "T"

How can Pittsburgh afford free transportation options?

Pittsburgh's light rail system, affectionately known as the "T," carries thousands of visitors and locals safely to their destinations each day. And, while you may have to pay a pretty penny to purchase transit cards to ride in other cities, Pittsburgh offers riders free passage to lessen boarding delays and encourage the use of city transit in specific areas of town.

It's absolutely true. If you're riding in the Golden Triangle area or to the North Shore and are staying within those particular boundaries, you can hop on and off as many times as you'd like free of charge. However, if you ride outside of those areas you will need to pay for tickets.

Although the trains may not show up, or leave, as quickly as the larger, bigger city trains in Manhattan or Chicago, the convenience truly does outweigh the lack. Plus, the trains, as well as the stops, are clean and safe.

There are six free stops total (five in downtown Pittsburgh, one on the North Shore), giving affordable means of travel to shoppers, people heading to games, or folks who want merely to look around the city. Many sports lovers choose to use a parking garage downtown and hop on the T to the North Shore as parking can get pretty expensive on that side of the Allegheny River.

The Pittsburgh Light Rail System has a total of 53 stations.

Gateway Station, one of several downtown Pittsburgh "T" stops. Photo credit: www.flickr.com/photos/parsonage1909/

But how does the city manage to keep the rides free? Happily, the Pittsburgh Steelers, Rivers Casino, and ALCO parking (all on the North Shore) all generously chip in and sponsor the charges to lessen the burden for city visitors. If you're over the age of 65 and have a SeniorConnect Card (or blue or yellow Pennsylvania Senior Citizen ID Card), you can ride for free anytime at any stop.

FREE PITTSBURGH TRANSPORTATION

WHAT Pittsburgh T

WHERE Golden Triangle and North Shore

COST Free

PRO TIP Especially for parades and holidays, park on the North Shore.

www.portauthority.org

WATERLOGGED

Why is a Pittsburgh theme park ride so beloved?

Right at the turn of the 20th century in the West Mifflin area of the city, Kennywood Park opened its gates for both amusement and escape from smog-filled Pittsburgh proper only a few miles away. From its place on the hill, views of the Carrie Furnace and Monongahela River can be spied from a few of its rides.

The park has continued to be a Pittsburgh summer theme park staple into the 21st century, including the "World's Oldest Continuously Operating Dark Water Ride." The Old Mill is the oldest ride in the park. Near the famous front tunnel entrance, it's easily located by its weathered wooden exterior and the scent of the water when you get close.

A replacement for one of its roller coasters, the Old Mill made its debut in 1901 to the delight of guests looking for indoor respite from the summer heat or a way to get a little closer to their dates. Rising to a maximum level of four feet, both gravity and water propulsion are responsible for getting boaters to their end destination safely.

And, while the Old Mill has undergone several theme changes throughout its 100-year run, fans of nostalgia still call it a Tunnel of Love even though it has hosted a lasagna-loving cat on a trippy 3D dream called "Garfield's Nightmare" since 2004. But, happily this year, the Old Mill is being renovated back to

OLDEST DARK WATER RIDE

WHAT Old Mill

WHERE Kennywood Park in West Mifflin

COST Adults $39.99, Children under 46 inches $34.99, Seniors 55+ $26.99, Military $28.00

PRO TIP The best time of day to visit Kennywood Park is when the park opens so you can take advantage of the lower numbers of people to hop on more rides.

www.kennywood.com

Photo of The Old Mill at Kennywood, which is being restored to its original theme in 2020! Photo credit: Nick Paradise/Kennywood Park

its former glory and original style. With a western-style theme comparable to the first theme, it will have some new, fun twists to keep the ride fresh with an old-school take. With glow in the dark paint, skeletons, and fun scenes, the ride will offer a "cozy up with your sweetheart" look and feel once more.

For 2020, Old Mill will officially lose its Garfield's Nightmare theme and go back to its original name.

THE PLUSH LIFE

How did the love of furry animal suits turn into a massive Pittsburgh convention?

If you've ever given a thought to what it would be like if animals walked, talked, and dressed like humans, you're definitely not alone. And furthermore, if you've given a second thought to humanizing animal cartoon characters or wanting to dress up like one, you're definitely among friends—once a year in Pittsburgh, that is.

For more than two decades, droves of humans dressed as animals (some with handlers due to the poor visibility the costumes provide), a.k.a. anthrocons, have flocked to downtown. They hang out at restaurants, chat with like-minded friends, and fill Pittsburgh hotels and their lobbies while staying in their character costumes.

Officially referred to as either Anthrocon or the Furry Convention, each summer this event attracts well over 8,000 folks from all over the world dressed as their favorite wolf, cat, dog, or any other animal you could imagine, to meet with like-minded (and like-dressed) enthusiasts to talk about art, discuss animation, or just hang out. You'll spy them walking the streets of downtown Pittsburgh, many times heading out for a bite to eat or to join up with friends, and for that week, dressing in costume becomes a way of life.

In addition to the camaraderie Anthrocon provides, seminars and workshops featuring everything from costume creation to writing take place to add to the furry fun and give guests their money's worth. And don't feel like you need to

Feel free to take photos of the Anthrocon furries—they didn't dress up for nothing!

A couple of the hundreds of furries that visit Anthrocon every year in Pittsburgh. Photo credit: www.flickr.com/photos/dmuth

dress as a character to take part in the fun: Out of curiosity, I've attended Anthrocon in the past and it was a hoot. The furries are more than happy to take photos and answer questions about their lifestyle. During First Night Pittsburgh, the local chapter even joins in on the New Year's Eve fun by marching in the parade in the Cultural District.

ANTHROCON

WHAT Pittsburgh's furry convention

WHERE David L. Lawrence Convention Center, 1000 Fort Duquesne Blvd.

COST $60 for a four-day pass

PRO TIP You don't have to have a costume to join in on the plushy, furry fun!

www.anthrocon.org

DEAD MEN WALKING

How does a cult-favorite horror movie inspire zombies to come out of hiding?

Each year, as a tribute to George Romero's *Night of the Living Dead* cult-classic horror film in which zombies were actually given free will for the first time, fans who love wearing shredded clothes piled over pasty makeup, barely blinking, and moving at a snail's pace turn up for the Zombie Walk and the creepy/cool events surrounding it.

It all started on September 29, 2006, at the Monroeville Mall where 900 "zombie" participants showed up to give props to both the movie genre and scary characters. Not only did they set a Guinness World Record for "Most People Participating in a Zombie Walk," the Pittsburgh Food Bank benefited from the large number of donations made to help the needy. Adding to the fun during the event, the zombies were asked to stay in character throughout, yet keep to a "Zombie Rules of Conduct" code.

Due to its popularity, the present-day Zombie Walk has been transformed into an entire festival called, what else? Zombie Fest. The undead event still offers a walk, but also amps up the creepy fun with a ball, concerts, a costume contest, and—most impressively—World Zombie Day that sheds light on world hunger.

ZOMBIE FEST AND ZOMBIE WALK

WHAT A way to channel your inner undead in Pittsburgh

WHERE Zombie Walk starts at Schenley Plaza, 4100 Forbes Ave.

COST Free

PRO TIP If you don't want to dress up like a creature of the undead, feel free to go to watch and take lots of photos.

www.pittsburghzombiefest.com

Such a sweet undead couple at Zombie Walk in Pittsburgh. Photo credit:
www.flickr.com/photos/daveynin/

The Pittsburgh Zombie Walk starts at 10 a.m.
sharp—no need for the dark of night for this crew.

NOT JUST NATURAL, *POST*NATURAL

How does a Pittsburgh museum shed light on genetic code alteration?

A goat that produces spider silk in its milk. A ribless mouse. A sterile Atlantic salmon with too many chromosomes. If you're intrigued by the oddities, you're not alone. Scientists at the Center for PostNatural History on Penn Avenue in Garfield are more than curious about the effects of human culture on these organisms that were intentionally and heritably altered by humans for education. Translation: each piece in the museum has had its genetic code deliberately altered for scientific purposes.

But why dedicate an entire museum to the modifications? For one, humans have always been curious about things they don't understand or know about (think about circus sideshows and their popularity), and secondly, there are enough exhibits and specimens at the Center to make anyone raise a skeptical eyebrow. In addition to its on-site education, the center offers traveling exhibits that were created to give off-site information to those who are just as curious as we are but can't make it to the museum or the city.

The Center was not created to sway opinions on the processes but merely to "acquire, interpret, and provide access" to organisms of postnatural origin. It's a fine line to

The Center is only open on Sundays, so please be sure to check the website or call ahead to verify times.

HALL OF POSTNATURAL HISTORY

OPEN

CENTER FOR
POSTNATURAL HISTORY

The only BioSteel™ Goat on public display in the entire world. Photo credit: Dror Yaron

THE CENTER FOR POSTNATURAL HISTORY

WHAT A genetic code alteration museum

WHERE 4913 Penn Ave.

COST Free

PRO TIP Go with an open mind, and feel free to donate if you enjoyed your visit.

www.postnatural.org

walk, but the Center does it very well. An informative way to spend an hour or two, it offers free admission to its guests (donations are always happily accepted) and a glimpse into both 20th century and modern scientific gene advancements. Plus, you may learn a thing or two about how (and why) scientists are altering genetic code in the first place.

THE BEST VIEW IN THE HOUSE, ER, CITY

Why is Pittsburgh's skyline view so famous?

The city of Pittsburgh offers a unique geography in that there are prominent rivers running along its downtown edges, surrounding it, and giving the city a distinct, compact layout. Add the fact that the city proper is situated in a large valley that is particularly beautiful during autumn and winter, and you're literally looking at a geographic and urban phenomenon.

Happily, city residents aren't the only ones who adore the view of the Pittsburgh skyline. Named "One of the Best Skyline Views in the World" by *USA Today* in 2014, the climb (whether by incline or car) up to Mt. Washington to see this famous view is well worth it, especially at night when the tall buildings are lit up. But the accolades don't end there: in 2013, the same newspaper awarded the city second place as one of the 10 Most Beautiful Places in America.

From 400 feet above the city's skyline, the Mt. Washington overlook provides an unobscured view of the skyscrapers, Point State Park, and the Sister Bridges. Hit the timing right during the day, and you can literally see the spot where the Allegheny and

PITTSBURGH SKYLINE

WHAT Best skyline view in the world

WHERE Mt. Washington

COST Free

PRO TIP The easiest way to climb the mountain is via an incline for a fee, but you can drive up and find parking.

Mt. Washington is a great place to watch holiday fireworks!

The jaw-dropping view of the Golden Triangle from Mount Washington. Photo credit: Steven Locke

Monongahela Rivers meet to form the Ohio River as a result of the difference between the two rivers' water colors.

And don't get me started on the four seasons' views of the city from high atop Mt. Washington. In autumn, the changing leaves, along with the fog that settles along the rivers on chilly mornings, make for gorgeous photos. And in winter, the snow covering the leafless trees, combined with the bright red and yellow of the Duquesne Incline trolleys, make for stunning views.

A GARDEN OF BIBLICAL PROPORTIONS

How does a Pittsburgh garden pay homage to the Holy Land?

Gently tucked in a busy area of town, the Ancient East meets the Western World at a beautiful spot on Fifth Avenue. The Rodef Shalom Biblical Botanical Garden is the only one of its kind—not only in Pittsburgh, but in the world—making it particularly unique to the city.

Opening in 1987 to guests, yearly theme changes keep guests both entertained and informed. Last year, a cooking theme (Food and Cooking in the First Diaspora) was added to the delight of visitors. With a deep respect for the Bible, and its devotees, it offers insight into the study of Middle Eastern agriculture and horticulture with special programs and plant additions.

This lovely garden does a great job of recreating the geography of the Holy Land and Ancient Israel, offering its guests a look at over 100 different plants that were mentioned in the Bible and even includes the verses where they were mentioned to correlate them. In addition to the biblical plants, the serene spot includes plants named after things or people from the Bible. To add to the beauty, small-scale biblical locations are showcased, including the River Jordan flowing from the Sea of Galilee to the Dead Sea, a desert scape, and even a pretty waterfall.

If you want to see the Biblical Botanical Garden in all its glory, you'll have to visit during warmer Pittsburgh months from early

---

Each season, a different theme involving Near Eastern horticulture is explored.

A Flowering Nile hosta at Rodef Shalom Biblical Botanical Garden. Photo credit: Nick Koehler

June through mid-September. Two-thirds of the garden's plants come from the Mediterranean Region of the world, and they're not fans of chilly Pittsburgh winters, so they have to be tended indoors until there's no threat of frost.

THE RODEF SHALOM BIBLICAL BOTANICAL GARDEN

WHAT A garden featuring plants named after (and found in) the Bible

WHERE 4905 5th Ave.

COST Free

PRO TIP The Garden is handicap accessible, and tours are offered the first Wednesday of every month at 12:15 p.m.

www.rodefshalom.org

WON'T YOU BE MY NORTH SHORE NEIGHBOR?

How does a hometown hero's statue still inspire kids today?

Throughout his adult life, Mister Fred Rogers prided himself on being a mere 143 pounds. In fact, he correlated the number with the phrase "I Love You" since the number of letters in each of the three words correlated to his weight: 1-4-3.

But to give the beloved children's television hero that small a tribute would never have worked in the city of Pittsburgh. Therefore, a 7,000-pound bronze statue given the fitting title *Tribute to Children* sits on the North Shore overlooking the Ohio River. Unveiled on November 5, 2009, it highlights a nostalgic moment from the show that children across the United States who watched it every day would have all been familiar with: Fred tying his shoes. Repurposing a pier from the torn-down Manchester Bridge, the piece cost $3 million to create, complete, and install.

Even though it is nearly 11 feet tall, you can actually walk right up, sit, and tie your shoes right alongside the man who taught you how during the opening minutes of every show. Or if you simply want to reflect on or enjoy the view of the three Pittsburgh rivers, follow Fred's advice and take 10 seconds to think of the people who helped you become who you are.

FRED ROGERS MEMORIAL STATUE

WHAT A larger-than-life tribute to Pittsburgh's hometown hero

WHERE North Shore near Carnegie Science Center, 1 Allegheny Ave.

COST Free

PRO TIP If you're feeling ambitious, visiting at sunrise or sunset makes for beautiful photos.

www.tributetochildren.org

Our hometown hero, larger than life, on the North Shore. Photo credit: Steven Locke

In 2015, a sound system was installed so visitors can listen to original Fred Rogers musical compositions.

SPEAK SLOW AND EASY AROUND THE OMNI WILLIAM PENN HOTEL

How did a former speakeasy turn into a popular bar today?

Long before the Prohibition era, Pittsburgh played an integral part in the Whiskey Rebellion in the late 1700s. In a nutshell, President Washington wanted to impose a liquor tax to decrease the national debt, but the city's local farmers and distillers weren't having it. To make a long story short, the federal government won, and the tax was levied. But Pittsburghers were still unhappy and continued to resist if anyone stepped between them and their libations of choice.

So, when laws were passed forbidding the selling of alcohol in the 1920s, Pittsburgh had its share of hidden bars selling illegal beverages, a.k.a. speakeasies. Given the title because of having to "speak slow and easy" about the underground lounges to thwart the police, speakeasies were all the rage due to Prohibition. In those days, folks donned their smartest outfits to enjoy the company of others and drink illegal booze.

At the Omni William Penn Hotel in downtown Pittsburgh, such a place existed on its lower level in the 1920s, but it had been used as a storage space for decades. In 2012, the space was completely overhauled to give the look and feel of what it may have looked like 100 years before. The bar now offers both traditional and modern cocktails and even has two whiskey bottles showcasing the original William Penn seals, a fun tie-in to the hotel's name.

The Omni William Penn turned 104 in 2020.

A modern take on an old-school hangout: the Speakeasy at the Omni William Penn Hotel. Photo credit: Steven Locke

But the coolest part is that the owners retained the second exit leading to Oliver Avenue in true speakeasy fashion. During Prohibition, the exit backup plan gave visitors a way to escape if the police raided the joint.

THE SPEAKEASY

WHAT A recreation of an actual speakeasy found at the Omni William Penn Hotel

WHERE 530 William Penn Pl.

COST Free to enter, but you'll definitely want one of its classic cocktails for the full experience. Prices vary.

PRO TIP The Speakeasy is open Tuesday through Thursday from 5 to 11 p.m. and weekends from 5 p.m. to 12:30 a.m.

www.omnihotels.com/hotels/pittsburgh-william-penn/dining/the-speakeasy

BURIED TO THEIR JOBS

Why are there cremains buried below a giant telescope?

Founded by several very rich industrialists in 1859, the Allegheny Telescope Association offered an official place to look at the stars and provide public education. In 1867, due to a lack of both money and membership, the Observatory was donated to the University of Pittsburgh, then known as Western University of Pennsylvania. Located in Riverview Park, just four miles north of downtown, the second, and final, version of the building took 12 years to complete, opening in 1912.

Now, when you visit the Allegheny Observatory, you can expect to see not only the stars and constellations but also multiple telescopes and additional celestial-gazing equipment in use to gain the best possible views.

But what you might not expect is the crypt located in the basement of the building. Right at the foot of Keeler Memorial Telescope's massive (in height, circumference, and capabilities) 31-inch-diameter mirror, lie the ashes of two prominent 19th- and 20th-century astronomers, John Brashear and James Edward Keeler, both observatory directors.

James Edward Keeler was the first to discover the gap in Saturn's rings known as the Encke Gap.

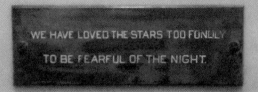

PHOEBE·S·BRASHEAR.
1843 — 1910.

WE HAVE LOVED THE STARS TOO FONDLY

TO BE FEARFUL OF THE NIGHT.

JOHN·A·BRASHEAR.
1840 — 1920.

Buried to their jobs at Allegheny Observatory? Literally, yes. Photo credit: www.flickr. com/photos/avicennasis/

But the men who loved their jobs so much that they wanted to remain there even in death aren't the only ones who have the Allegheny Observatory as their final resting place: both Brashear's and Keeler's wives, along with Keeler's son, Henry, asked for their remains to be placed there as well.

UNDERWATER SUBMERSIBLE IN THE OHIO

How did a military submarine end up on Pittsburgh's North Shore?

When you think of submarines, do you picture them hundreds of feet below the water in a giant sea or ocean, filled with both high-tech equipment and military men and/or women enlisted to defend their country? For many of us, that scenario is what comes to mind thanks to old war stories, movies, and TV shows.

However, USS *Requin*, a 312-foot-long, Tench-class submarine, breaks that stereotype by sitting quietly half above and half below the water right off the riverbank outside of the Carnegie Science Center on the North Shore. As such, USS *Requin* missed out on the military battles. Scheduled for official duty on August 21, 1945, World War II ended a week before the *Requin* and its crew were deemed ready to take on the enemy.

Today, USS *Requin* graces the shores of the Ohio River to educate Carnegie Science Center visitors about the life and necessity of a 20th-century submarine and to highlight how far we've come in the creation of modern-day, nuclear-powered subs.

USS *REQUIN*

WHAT Military submarine at Carnegie Science Center

WHERE Carnegie Science Center, 1 Allegheny Ave.

COST Adults $19.95, Seniors (65+) $14.95, Children 3-18 $11.95, Children under 2 and Members Free.

PRO TIP Self-guided tours are included in CSC admission, so make sure to tour all of the Center to get your money's worth.

www.carnegiesciencecenter.org

A pretty view of downtown Pittsburgh from the view of USS Requin. *Photo credit: Steven Locke*

USS *Requin* weighs 2,414 tons submerged.

WAIT A 35-FOOT MINUTE!

How did a prominent Pittsburgh clock end up changing hands so often?

Let's consider all the giant clocks from all over the world. There's the Mecca Royal Clock Tower in Saudi Arabia; the Floral Clock in Surat, India; and the Istanbul Cevahir clock that's at the top of the list. But did you know that Pittsburgh's Coca-Cola Clock on the corner of Mary and 21st Streets is the largest single-face clock in the United States, not to mention the fifth largest clock in the world?

What started out as a billboard for the popular carbonated beverage in 1933 has changed hands a few times. It belonged to the Duquesne Brewing Company in 1961 and to WTAE in the 1970s. The clock's octagonal face measures 60-by-60 feet, has a 25-foot-long hour hand, and a whopping 35-foot minute hand.

The clock's last advertising ownership officially belonged to AT&T, who gave the clock a blue and white paint job in 2009 to match its familiar logo. As of 2017 the clock face is mostly painted gray and offers no advertising—but it still keeps the correct time of day.

PITTSBURGH'S COCA-COLA CLOCK

WHAT Largest Single-Face Clock in the United States

WHERE Duquesne Brewery building, 181 S. 21st St.

COST Free to view and take photos

PRO TIP The clock is an icon of Pittsburgh's landscape—make sure to take plenty of photos.

When installed, the Pittsburgh Coca-Cola Clock was the largest single-faced clock in the world.

The famous Coca-Cola Clock on Pittsburgh's South Side. Photo credit: Steven Locke

No matter who or what maintains responsibility for the giant timepiece, it will always be known to old-school Pittsburghers as the Coca-Cola Clock.

UNUSUAL "MANOR"ISMS

How did a love for the macabre turn into a curiosity museum?

Creepy? Sure. Quirky? Definitely. Unusual? Absolutely! If we were limited to only three words to describe Trundle Manor in Swissvale, creepy, quirky, and unusual would do nicely. But the privately owned home and museum is so much more than just a salute to all things odd. Built in 1910, the Victorian-style dwelling is ideal in both architecture and decor for such a collection with its various nooks and crannies; just the place for a "singing" tumor donated by a belly dancer.

Around every corner, and in every nook and cranny they could find, there are wall-to-wall pieces, including their beloved cat, Little Devil, now taxidermied and placed in a glass cabinet as tribute. Ask them about their taxidermy collection and you'll understand why they collect the pieces—to keep them from going into the trash at other homes and to put them in a spot that will keep them safe and admired.

Owned by Mr. Arm and Velda Von Minx (a.k.a. Anton and Rachel Mirello), the self-professed tourist trap harbors a

TRUNDLE MANOR

WHAT Museum of Oddities

WHERE 7724 Juniata St.

COST Free but donations (both cash and liquor!) are accepted

PRO TIP Tours are available by appointment only and last approximately one hour. You'll need to either email or text Trundle Manor to make arrangements.

www.trundlemanor.com

Trundle Manor has unusual items outside as well, including the Mobile Office of Villainy in a former cable repair truck.

Whether it's an old, creepy chair in the kitchen or an even creepier skeleton in the living room, Trundle Manor has plenty of oddities to spy. Photo credit: Steven Locke

variety of taxidermy animals, a jar collection filled with once-living specimens and their parts, and even a coffin if you're inclined to take a spin inside. Open to the public since 2009, Trundle Manor has been a place for the Mirellos to amass their unusual collection and showcase their artistic talents, which grew out of a love of classic goth and horror films.

The Mirellos love giving house tours in full costume, but you'll have to make an appointment as drop-ins are not allowed. There is no cost for touring the property, but donations are recommended: gifts can range from cash to booze to adding a fitting item to their collection.

MAD FOR MUSIC BOXES

How did a love of music boxes turn into a full-fledged museum?

Taking a cue from the British, *mad* actually means "crazy about," so a man mad for music boxes is definitely a wonderful thing, yes? On a hill in O'Hara Township sits a 19,000-square-foot mansion built by Charles Brown III. Its completion in 1982 made for a giant, quirky space to house Brown's passion for collectibles and unique takes on living-space decor. This space, the Baynerhof, is considered one of the true hidden gems in Pittsburgh and for good reason.

His love of the ornate boxes evolved into a passion for collecting larger, more complex antique music machines, and eventually his mansion became not only a place to enjoy the company of friends, but an adventure-filled evening tour for all invited guests as well.

To this day, the Bayernhof Museum houses all the items that Mr. Brown enjoyed in life, including a cave fashioned after Carlsbad Caverns that leads straight to an indoor swimming pool room. Luckily (for us), Chuck Brown donated his dwelling to a foundation that's happy to keep both his mansion and music boxes in tip-top shape.

Standout pieces include the giant Hupfeld Phonoliszt Violina that plays three violins and an upright piano simultaneously, along with more understated pieces such as the delicate Bird Box created in 1848.

BAYERNHOF MUSEUM

WHAT Antique music machine museum

WHERE 225 St. Charles Pl.

COST $10 per person

PRO TIP Tours are guided, offered by appointment only, and must be scheduled before arriving.

www.bayernhofmuseum.com

One of the many music boxes at Bayernhof Museum. Photo credit: www.flickr.com/photos/nlgconsulting/

Bayernhof music boxes require constant maintenance and upkeep.

THE GINCH WHO COLLECTS MUSICAL MEMORABILIA

How did a popular Pittsburgh musician create a hip place to showcase his rock and roll memorabilia?

Bad. Sick. Cool. Hip. Awesome. Hot.

If you're not from the mid-20th century or earlier, you may not have heard the adjective that encompasses all of the above ("ginchy"), and you probably have not ever uttered the word. But Jack Hunt, a.k.a. Johnny Halo, a Pittsburgh musical icon and the man who—along with his band—makes everyone happy on the dance floor, are quintessential ginchy, man. Attend one of his local shows filled with throwback hits and a fun vibe, and you'll understand why.

Johnny Angel's Ginchy Stuff on the Northside houses a ton of cool memorabilia that the singer has collected throughout his musical career. Along with a plethora of autographed photos from celebrities and personalized letters to Angel, you'll also find plenty of retro-style items for sale, making it part shop, part museum.

JOHNNY ANGEL'S GINCHY STUFF

WHAT Rock and roll memorabilia store

WHERE 1800 Preble Ave.

COST Free

PRO TIP The store/museum is open every day but Mondays and Tuesdays.

www.jaginchystuff.com

Johnny Angel and the Halos have been playing since 1972.

Old-school cool at Johnny Angel's Ginchy Stuff. Photo credit: www.flickr.com/photos/ the-spoon

This treasure trove of musical collectibles makes a visit to Ginchy Stuff feel like having a walk-on part in an episode of *This Is Your Life, Johnny Angel* or taking a trip down memory lane for Pittsburgh band lovers. But, if you really want to laugh, visit with the kids or grandkids and show them vinyl records or a cassette tape. You'll either feel highly knowledgeable or really old.

RANDY WITH ART

How did a man with a budget of a few thousand dollars turn a rundown house into a place of inspiration?

The Northside of Pittsburgh is known for its eclectic and quirky shops, cool brew pubs, beautiful outdoorsy spots, and museums along some pretty narrow streets. But the part-art-museum, part-creative-inspiration spot, Randyland, is not only eclectically quirky, it's also become a place of smiles and happiness for its visitors. Dubbed the Most Colorful Place in Pittsburgh, owner Randy Gilson's labor of artistic love began in 1995 when he bought the property at auction for $10,000 on his credit card.

In the beginning, Randy wasn't sure what would become of the rundown building sitting on the corner of Jacksonia and Arch Streets, but his love of colorful art and making people smile turned it into the coolest, brightest collection of junk you've ever seen in Pittsburgh.

Not only does Randy himself paint items, he encourages visitors to grab a paint brush and get creative right along with him. Randyland's message is simple: "happiness shouldn't

RANDYLAND

WHAT Pittsburgh's most colorful art

WHERE 1501 Arch St.

COST Free but donations happily accepted

PRO TIP If you want to leave your mark on Randyland, pull some inspirations from your surroundings and create by painting or making your own piece of art.

https://randy.land

Randy Gilson was featured in WQED's *The Spirit of Pittsburgh* showcasing "guerilla gardening" tips.

Someone's trash becomes Randy Gilson's treasure at Randyland on the Northside.
Photo credit: Steven Locke

cost anything," and his way of upcycling and repurposing junk puts brightness into many of the overcast days that Pittsburgh residents have learned to endure. And it's this constant evolution of Randyland that allows folks to gain inspiration from it in a different way each time they visit.

SECOND TO THE VATICAN

Where can you find the largest collection of religious relics in the world outside of the Vatican?

In the middle of the 19th century, the wealthy Belgian aristocrat, Suitbert Godfrey Mollinger, made a trip around Europe in between graduating from school and attending university. It was then that he chose his first profession: medicine. In 1852, he began training for his second calling: the priesthood.

Recruited for American mission work, Father Mollinger began collecting religious relics that were destined to be sold or destroyed because of the anti-Catholic campaigns all over Europe. Catholics actually sought out Mollinger and, before he knew it, he had amassed over 5,000 relics. By then, he had settled in Pittsburgh.

The priest actually had to pay out of his own pocket for a new chapel to be built because his collection has grown so large. Hence, St. Anthony's Chapel in Troy Hill stands peacefully on a quiet spot on Harpster Street in honor of both the priest and his priceless assemblage.

While each relic has its own story, the Chapel's most famous pieces are a tooth from patron saint Anthony of Padua

ST. ANTHONY'S CHAPEL

WHAT Largest collection of religious relics outside of the Vatican

WHERE 1704 Harpster St.

COST Donations accepted

PRO TIP St. Anthony's Chapel is open every day but Fridays and does not allow photos, making it an ideal place to just be present and in the moment.

saintanthonyschapel.org

The bones of St. Frances of Rome (No. 236), dated August 12, 1716, is the oldest exhibit in the St. Anthony relic collection.

Just a few of the thousands of religious relics at St. Anthony's Chapel. Photo credit: www.flickr.com/photos/emmandevin

(for whom the chapel was named) and a thorn reputed to be from the crown of thorns woven for Jesus Christ by Roman soldiers during his crucifixion.

It's here that Father Mollinger both blessed and/or healed thousands of petitioners with both prayers and medicine, combining his skills. These days, visiting the Chapel has become a pilgrimage for many of the faithful who come to pray or view the relics, museum-style.

YOU LOOK SMASHING, ATOM

Where can you see the remnants of a giant atom smasher?

Remember the elementary school science experiment where all of your classmates would gather around an electrified sphere, grab it with their hands, and feel their hair stand on end (especially the kids with super fine hair), much to the delight and giggles of their peers?

What was once a scientific learning tool about static electricity became part of a large-scale nuclear physics research location in Forest Hills. The fancy name for the large static ball is a Van De Graff generator and its ties to Pittsburgh are absolutely smashing, baby.

In a nutshell, it used an endless belt made from rubber or fabric (think about rubbing a balloon over a wool carpet when you were a kid to get it to stick to the wall) to make electrical charges. Sending those charges to a roller at its base, the charges were deposited into a hollowed, metal electrode at the top. Between the two electrodes at top and bottom, high voltage electricity was created.

At 65 feet tall, the Westinghouse Atom Smasher was easy to spot in Forest Hills. You couldn't help but see what looked like a giant light bulb growing out of the top of a building from just about anywhere you were in the area.

The "centerpiece of the first large-scale program in nuclear physics established in industry," it was in operation from 1937 to 1958 and remained part of the Forest Hills skyline until the mid-2010s when it was knocked down by a land developer. Despite a promised restoration, the Van de Graaff Generator is still lying on its side waiting for a new base before it can be returned it to its iconic spot.

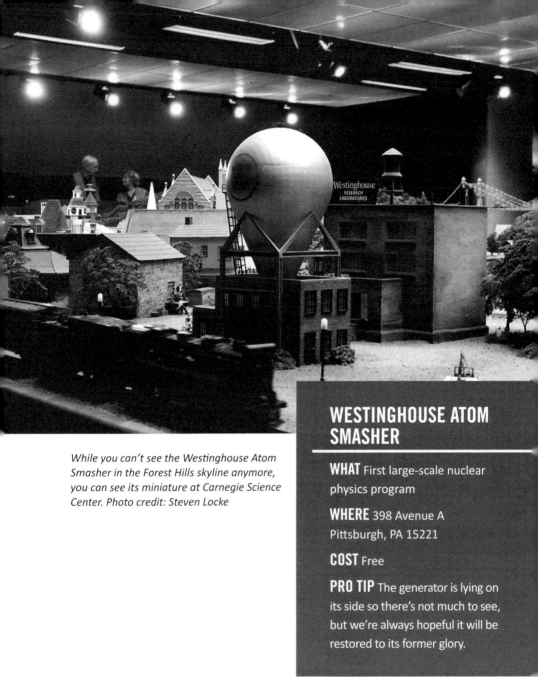

While you can't see the Westinghouse Atom Smasher in the Forest Hills skyline anymore, you can see its miniature at Carnegie Science Center. Photo credit: Steven Locke

WESTINGHOUSE ATOM SMASHER

WHAT First large-scale nuclear physics program

WHERE 398 Avenue A Pittsburgh, PA 15221

COST Free

PRO TIP The generator is lying on its side so there's not much to see, but we're always hopeful it will be restored to its former glory.

The Westinghouse Atom Smasher has a scaled replica at Carnegie Science Center's *Miniature Railroad & Village*® exhibit.

PITTSBURGH'S PATRON SPONSORS DIPPY DINO

How did a giant dinosaur fossil get named after a Pittsburgh philanthropist?

The famous Scottish steel tycoon, Andrew Carnegie, was not only brilliant at making money, he was a philanthropist who felt a moral obligation to give large amounts of his money to good causes. Happily, in 1902, he founded the Carnegie Museum of Natural History in Oakland to give back to the community with scientific research, and that included digging for dinosaurs, a.k.a., archaeology.

As a tribute to Carnegie, the first dinosaur to be collected for the Museum in 1899 in Sheep Creek, Wyoming, was named after him: *Diplodocus carnegii*. Given the nickname "Dippy," the fossilized dinosaur became an instant celebrity as dinosaurs go, and several plaster casts were made of his bones, which allowed the dinosaur's remains to be made available for viewing all over the world. For many, it was the first dinosaur they'd ever seen, and both the original fossil and casts were met with delight. Eventually, Dippy became the focus piece in the Carnegie Museum as a result of an expansion.

One hundred years later in 1999, a giant cartoon-like version of Dippy the Dinosaur became a prominent figure in front of the Carnegie Music Hall entrance. In keeping with Carnegie's passion for learning about evolution, the statue is 22 feet long, 84 feet high, and weighs a massive 3,000 pounds in fiberglass and paint.

DIPPY THE DINOSAUR

WHAT Carnegie Museum's giant diplodocus statue

WHERE Carnegie Museum of Natural History, 4400 Forbes Ave.

COST Free

PRO TIP Dippy hangs out near the entrance to Carnegie Music Hall—you can't miss him!

https://carnegiemnh.org/discovering-dippy

A cool photo spot in Oakland is in front of Dippy the Dinosaur. Photo credit: Steven Locke

It took 130 large crates to ship Dippy's bones to the museum.

MAN OF STEEL

How did a mythical man of steel become the icon for one of Pittsburgh's prominent steel mills?

In the 1930s when the Pittsburgh steel industry was booming and causing the city proper to be blanketed with blue dust, a mythical hero was born: Mighty Joe Magarac. He was given superhero qualities that could give modern-day heroes a run for their money: born in an iron mine, he would stir molten metal with his fists, form cannon balls with his bare hands, and squeeze steel railroad rails by merely pressing molten metal between his fingers. He was the epitome of everything a good steel worker could be, and he never took any time off.

In fact, mythical Magarac, whose last name literally translates to "donkey" in Croatian, never missed a day working in the mill and, at his triumphant end, sacrificed himself by jumping into a vat of molten steel to create "the finest steel ever produced"—only to be made into another steel mill.

Whether he was idolized by Pittsburgh steelworkers is still up for debate, but a tribute to Mighty Joe Magarac still stands outside of US Steel's Edgar Thomson Works in Braddock as a memory of the hard times local steelworkers faced. Over the years, the statue has been given several touch-up paint jobs for his clothing, skin, and hair, but these days he dons a pair of red pants with a blue shirt and is otherwise silver in tone to pay homage to shiny steel.

JOE MAGARAC STATUE

WHAT A tribute to the mythical steel worker superhero

WHERE 152 11th St., Braddock

COST Free

PRO TIP Mighty Joe is definitely a cool statue to check out, even if only once.

The Mighty Joe Magarac tribute at US Steel's Edgar Thomson Works. Photo credit: Steven Locke

The Magarac statue showcases the steel mill icon bending a bar of steel with his bare hands.

EMERALD RING AROUND THE NEIGHBORS

How did three Pittsburgh neighborhoods come together to make a picturesque park?

The quaint, adjacent neighborhoods of Mt. Washington, Duquesne Heights, and Allentown have the best view of the Pittsburgh skyline. But locals with a dream of having a place for themselves and their families to hang out and enjoy that view combined already-developed park space with the hillsides of Mr. Washington that had been mined for coal and created the new-and-improved Emerald View Park.

The 257-acre greenspace comprises serene spots, art pieces that can withstand Pittsburgh's four seasons, and quiet places to rest or reflect, as well as hiking and walking trails. Officially opened to the public on Earth Day 2007, what was once an overused eyesore and dump site for unwanted items and large pieces of junk became an outdoor haven for all to enjoy.

So, why did the neighborhoods combine to make one large greenspace and why the name Emerald View Park? A

EMERALD VIEW PARK

WHAT A greenspace created from mined hillsides

WHERE Bailey Ave.

COST Free

PRO TIP If you're able, visit Emerald Park on a clear, sunny day for gorgeous views of the Pittsburgh skyline.

www.pittsburghparks.org/emerald-view-park

There are several hidden surprises inside the park, including Depression-era sandstone walls and steps.

While we can only guess at how the name Emerald View Park came to be, we don't have to for its location. Photo credit: Steven Locke

fluke tornado in June 1998 caused a lot of damage. This gave the community an opportunity to rally and to work out a plan to clean up the dumpsites, restore the natural park habitats, clear miles of trails, and make capital improvements. As for the name, we can only guess that it has something to do with the foliage additions and lovely view of the city proper, or maybe the fact that the three areas were strung together like an emerald necklace.

MURALS TO THE MAX(O)

Where can you see church walls adorned with not-so-religious works of art?

The first Croatian church ever to be established in America just happened to be in the Bennett Hill area in Millvale. Seeking the American dream of prosperity, the area's Croatian immigrants began working in the local steel mills or mines. As a tribute to their homeland and needing a place for worship, St. Nicholas Croatian Catholic Church was built in honor of Sveti Nicola, a Saint who brings children gifts in early December after leaving their freshly polished boots on the windowsill.

All was well up until 1921 when a catastrophic fire demolished the church to the point where it had to be rebuilt. Happily, a brand-new church was completed, dedicated, and ready for worshipers in 1922, although its walls weren't adorned with paintings or religious murals for about 15 years. St. Nicholas's walls remained plain until a contract was made between Father Albert Zagar and Croatian artist, Maxo Vanka. During two visits in 1937 and 1941, Vanka completed 25 murals showcasing his beliefs on everything from social injustice to war—not your typical church topics.

Vanka continued to decorate the church with intricate textile designs and to add five symbols of Christianity to its choir loft as his gift to America. Although St. Nicholas is still an active church, docent-led tours are given to visitors wanting to see and learn more about this creative Croatian artist.

MAXO VANKA MURALS

WHAT Paintings on the walls of St. Nicholas Croatian Catholic Church

WHERE 24 Maryland Ave.

COST $10 per person

PRO TIP Tours are given on Saturdays, last around an hour, and give insight into the artist and his work.

https://vankamurals.org

Details for days on every Maxo Vanka mural in St. Nicholas Croatian Catholic Church. Photo credit: www.flickr.com/photos/smallcurio/

In 1981, Vanka was memorialized in the play, *Gift to America*, written by a Carnegie Mellon University professor.

THIS ZOO'S FOR THE BIRDS

Where is the only zoo solely dedicated to our feathered friends?

With more than 500 flying creatures representing 150 species, the National Aviary on the Northside is literally for the birds. Offering guests a glimpse at both common and rare, endangered species, don't be surprised if you get buzzed from above during your visit as many of the birds are allowed free flight in a couple of its giant rooms. To add to the interactive experience, the Aviary offers encounters meant to give insight into the habits of the animals it harbors including nonflying types such as sloths and armadillos. During an encounter, these animal ambassadors give a glimpse into how they move, eat, and interact with their same species and with humans. Yes, each encounter is an additional charge from basic admission, but the close encounters are worth every penny, as the money goes straight back into the zoo. If you're not a fan of up-close views, several of its birds have been trained to hold a paintbrush and literally paint on canvas, making the art one of a kind.

But what makes the National Aviary particularly special and sets it apart from a traditional zoo? Not only was it one of the first to offer free-flight rooms, it also happens to be the only indoor nonprofit zoo dedicated exclusively to birds in America.

NATIONAL AVIARY

WHAT Only indoor nonprofit zoo dedicated to birds

WHERE 700 Arch St.

COST Adults $17, Children ages 2-12 $16, Seniors $16

PRO TIP The National Aviary offers viewing both inside and out, so dress appropriately.

www.aviary.org

The National Aviary has the world's only indoor, free-flight, bird-show theater.

An Inca Tern, one of 150 species of birds at National Aviary. Photo credit: Steven Locke

A real draw is its penguin exhibit, *Penguin Point*. Featuring 16 African penguins, it offers a 360-degree view of our waddling feathered friends with several of them named after prominent players and staff on the city's hockey team, the Pittsburgh Penguins. If you can't make it to see them in person, no worries: the Aviary offers a Penguin Nest Cam on its website with a live feed highlighting newly hatched chicks.

A JAW-DROPPING FRONT DOOR

Where can you see Pittsburgh through a massive front door?

As you're driving into the heart of the downtown areas of most major cities, you can begin to see glimpses of the city proper and its skyline from your car window. And, whether it's your first time visiting a city or your hundredth, many times the view is a glimpse of what's to come. But downtown Pittsburgh makes a dramatic appearance in the light at the end of a tunnel with no sneak peak whatsoever.

Have you ever opened a door, only to spy a breathtaking view that makes your jaw drop? For Pittsburgh residents and visitors, the city's inbound Fort Pitt Tunnel, a.k.a. Parkway West, offers visitors one of the best "front door" views of any city skyline around.

And there's no hint or tease of what's to come, no spying prominent skyscrapers in the distance because the tunnel blocks them out. However, as soon as you exit the mile-long, two-lane tunnel, the whole of Pittsburgh opens up before you, providing a stunning view of its green spaces, tall office buildings, and impressive skyline—all at 55 m.p.h. There is a running joke about that end, though: once exited, you'll need to pay more attention to the road than the view if you're driving because many times merging into a different lane is a must.

And no matter how long drivers have to wait to get into Fort Pitt Tunnel (it's also been ranked one of the most

---

On average, 28 accidents occur in the Fort Pitt Tunnels every week.

A city with a front door view? Yes, and Pittsburgh's got the best one. Photo credit: Steven Locke

THE PITTSBURGH SKYLINE

WHAT Best front door view of a city

WHERE Downtown Pittsburgh via Fort Pitt Tunnel

COST Free

PRO TIP If you want a photo of the best front door view, make sure to let your passenger do the honors. As soon as you're out of the tunnels, traffic can get iffy.

congested roads in the country), there's no denying that seeing the Pittsburgh Welcome Mat, a.k.a., Point State Park, was worth the stagnant, stop-and-go traffic to get there.

IN-HOUSE PUBLICATIONS

Where can you check out written works painted on the sides of homes?

The controversial act of book burning to censor and stifle what people were allowed to read has been recorded since as early as 211 BCE. But what if, instead of just burning an author's writings, a full-out assassination plan was put in place?

Sadly, we'd like to think that was just a wicked fairy tale, but it's absolutely true. Assassination plans continue to happen in the present day, and controversial writers must look for asylum, many times thousands of miles from their native lands. Major expenses are incurred for travel and safety, not to mention major stress, so writers on the run may live in poverty for simply speaking their minds or giving true accounts about what goes on in their countries.

CITY OF ASYLUM HOUSE PUBLICATIONS

WHAT Decorated homes for artists seeking asylum in Pittsburgh

WHERE Sampsonia Way

COST Free

PRO TIP You'll definitely want to slow your roll and walk along Sampsonia Way to really get the vibe and feel of the homes.

Happily, in Pittsburgh, there's a company that gives hope to artists on the run. The City of Asylum, Pittsburgh chapter, offers both freedom of speech and publication to hosted writers, as well as physical safety. And it's been doing so since 2004.

Not only do the writers continue to create and find inspiration in the city, but Sampsonia Way on the Northside is the place they've been calling home with colorfully adorned Published Homes—commissioned exterior artwork that features the artist-in-residence's written work. The "public library" not only upgrades the houses, it brings beauty and positive cultural integration to the street.

One of four beautifully painted Published Homes on the North Shore. Photo credit: Steven Locke

At present, four Published Homes can be viewed with an additional house currently in rehabilitation.

INVENTION INCUBATION

Where can you see a fairy-tale setting made for invention?

As the truthful old saying goes, necessity is the mother of invention. If you've come up with a brilliant product that would make everyone's lives easier and want to get it into the hands of buyers, how or where do you even begin to start creating, designing, and bringing your idea to fruition?

Here in the Steel City, you need look no further than InventionLand, a 60,000-square-foot immersive workspace. This company is all about promoting innovation and inspiring people to build their dream product.

And if educational fostering weren't enough, the folks who get to call working at InventionLand their job have a storybook setting, literally: the company offers 16 themed areas where the invention magic begins. Working out plans for a children's product? The Nursery Nook is the place where you'll find inspiration. Need a Zen moment to balance out a stressful day of planning? Creation Cavern with a built-in waterfall is a peaceful place to park yourself and relax.

Happily, loads of products have made their way onto store shelves including a Half N Half cupcake pan, a locking soda can (or, if you're from

INVENTIONLAND

WHAT A massive invention creation space

WHERE 585 Alpha Dr.

COST Free

PRO TIP There are no walk-in tours; you'll need to schedule one ahead of time.

https://inventionland.com

There are 15 unique departments inside InventionLand.

Inspiration for tech products and games, it's Pirate Ship Discovery in InventionLand.
Photo credit: www.flickr.com/photos/nlgconsulting

Pittsburgh, pop can) top to keep your beverage pleasantly fizzy, and wireless turn-signal mirrors. You don't have to have a better mousetrap idea to get inside and take a peek around, either. InventionLand offers scheduled guest tours throughout the workweek. Of course, you'll have to sign a confidentiality waiver when you do—no one wants their better mousetrap idea out in the open before its due time.

ORIGINAL OYSTER HOUSE (page 128)

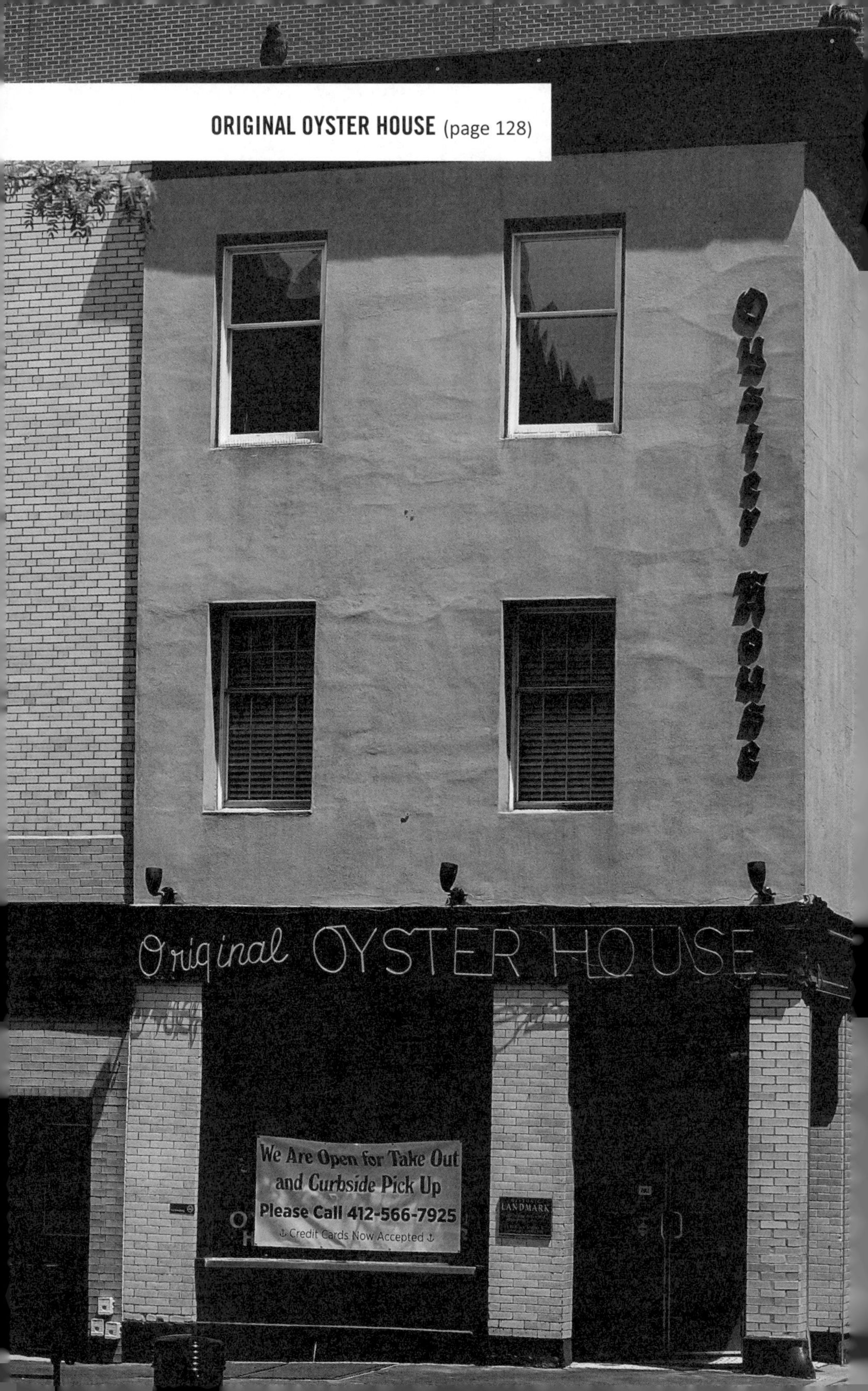

EMERALD VIEW PARK (page 74)

CLOUDY PITTSBURGH (page 114)

FERRIS WHEEL (page 24)

HAND-CRAFTED COCKTAIL
BUTCHER AND THE RYE
212 SIXTH STREET / PITTSBURGH, PA

CREATED BY: Lemon Passion

NO. 14

BUTCHER AND THE RYE (page 132)

NEIGHBORHOOD OF MAKE-BELIEVE (page 30)

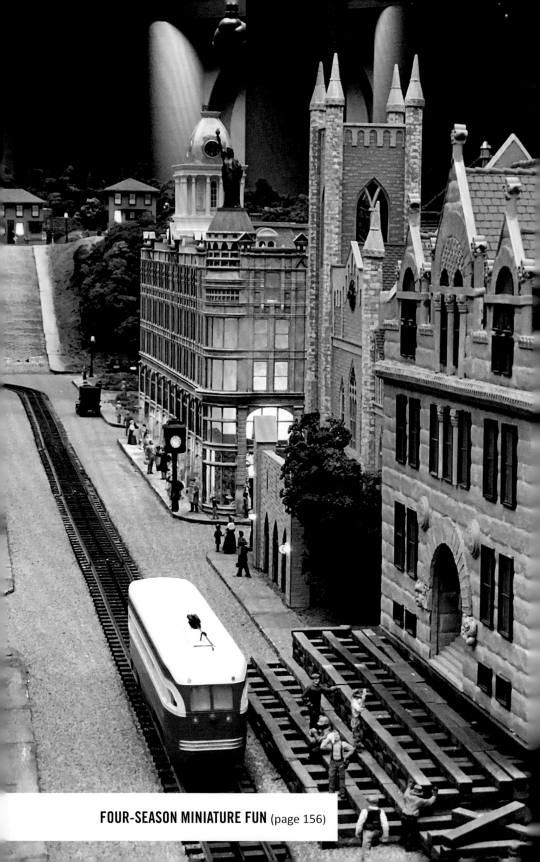

FOUR-SEASON MINIATURE FUN (page 156)

RANDYLAND (page 64)

MARY KRAMER
APR 13 1843
AUG 13 1896

ALICE KRAMER
APR 18 1873
MAY 18 1854

EVANS CITY CEMETERY (page 166)

IMMACULATE DOMINATION (page 140)

IT'S A BIRD! IT'S A PLANE! IT'S… AN ACORN? (page 172)

THE KRAUS CAMPO (page 182)

ANDY WARHOL'S GRAVE (page 106)

RUST BELT BEAUTY

Where can you tour historical sites that offer a glimpse into Pittsburgh's Rust Belt?

During the 20th century, the borough of Rankin, a western neighborhood of Pittsburgh situated along the Monongahela River, was a hustling, bustling community thanks to the steel mill industry. Sadly, as with many cities dominated by steel mills as a main source of income during the late 1970s and early 1980s, most of the mills in Pittsburgh were forced to close, often without much notice to their workers. Former factory employees were forced to either look for lower-paying jobs or move to a new city completely.

The beautiful Carrie Furnace, part of Homestead Steel Works, made its last run in 1982 and became part of the "Rust Belt" that stretched from Wisconsin through Pennsylvania due to the resulting economic decline. Most of the site has been torn down, but furnaces #6 and 7, which offer a glimpse into the formerly thriving area, are still on-site and their beauty is worthy of an Instagram post.

Instead of focusing on the bad side, Rivers of Steel offers tours and insights into the power of repurposing the Carrie

---

CARRIE FURNACE

WHAT A Pittsburgh steel mill offering insight into the Rust Belt

WHERE 801 Carrie Furnace Blvd., Rankin

COST Adults $21, Students 18+ (with ID) and Seniors 62+ $17, Children 4-17 $14

PRO TIP Make sure to wear closed-toed shoes—you'll be doing a lot of walking and stair climbing.

www.riversofsteel.com

When in peak production, the Carrie Blast Furnace produced more than 1,000 tons of iron each day.

All the rust belt beauty at Carrie Furnace. Photo credit: Steven Locke

Furnaces by showing how nature reclamation works in the post-industrial landscape. This former factory site has also been the home of morning yoga sessions followed by a beer at the local brew pub to encourage young adults to give back to the community. And instead of erasing decades-old graffiti painted by known local artists, legal graffiti walls are available to give a street-art timeline to its visitors.

24/7 "SOUP"ER CEMETERY

Where can you see the grave of a Pittsburgh art icon?

On August 6, 1928, Andrew Warhola was born in a two-bedroom apartment to Carpatho-Rusyn (Eastern Slovakia) immigrant parents. Lacking the finer things in life during the Depression era, Warhola found amusement with comic books, simple paper cutouts, and free art classes. His father helped his son's talent blossom by saving money to pay for his college education at Carnegie Institute of Technology.

After dropping the second "a" in his last name, Pittsburgh's art hero, Andy Warhol, was ready to take the art world by storm with his creative, unique spin on both common life and celebrities. His most famous piece is simply titled *Campbell's Soup Cans* from 1962.

Sadly, after bladder surgery complications, Warhol passed away at the relatively young age of 58 and was buried in Saint John the Baptist Byzantine Catholic Cemetery in Bethel Park. His final resting place is visited frequently by his fans and art lovers, many times with the famous cans brought and set on his headstone as a tribute.

And if a visit to his final resting place isn't enough, two 24-hour webcams run by the Andy Warhol Museum let us spy on the grave, local weather conditions, and folks who simply want to pay their respects.

ANDY WARHOL'S GRAVE

WHAT Warhol's final resting place and spot for fans to visit to pay their respects

WHERE 1050-1060 Connor Rd., Castle Shannon

COST Free

PRO TIP If you want to leave a can of Campbell's soup on the grave as a tribute, it's absolutely okay.

www.warhol.org/andy-warhols-life/figment

Constant tributes for Andy Warhol's grave, including a soup can donning a face mask.
Photo credit: Steven Locke

The Warhol grave cam is titled *Figment* after a quote by the artist stating that the word should be the only thing written on his headstone.

A LIGHT DISPLAY TO MAKE CLARK GRISWOLD GREEN WITH ENVY

Where can you see a Christmas-style light display sensational enough to make Clark Griswald envious year-round?

There's a place near Pittsburgh where Margaritaville meets Mid-America, and that is Bob's Garage in Blawnox. The one-story bar looks like almost all the other stand-alone Pittsburgh bars on the outside except for one major thing: it has a massive holiday light display that looks like something out of *National Lampoon's Christmas Vacation*.

Each quarter, the colorful displays and kitschy decorations get changed out to fit the current holiday theme—which is one heck of a feat—but it's the Christmas season where the bar proverbially, as well as literally, shines. That season lasts from November through February to give folks enough time to celebrate with Bob.

BOB'S GARAGE LIGHT DISPLAY

WHAT A restaurant/bar with thousands of Christmas lights year-round

WHERE 1372 Freeport Rd.

COST Free

PRO TIP It's fine if you want to do a drive-by viewing, but if you really want to get the feel for Bob's vibe, step up to the bar and hang with the locals.

www.facebook.com/Bobs-Garage-126837474022267

Are the drinks overpriced? Probably. But what you get in addition to cocktails and brews is a fun ambiance that makes you feel like you're in Vegas. It's so much fun that there are regulars who have made the hangout a weekly destination.

Clark Griswald has nothing on Bob's Garage, especially during the winter holidays.
Photo credit: Pixabay

But what really illuminates the Christmas spirit is the generosity from both owner, Bob Pagliano, and his staff. Pagliano has established the nonprofit organization Spirit of Christmas, to give much-appreciated help to needy families in the area. Upwards of 350 families are given holiday assistance each season from the Spirit of Christmas fund, making it even more worth your while to spend money on a trip to Bob's.

An estimate of the number of Christmas lights at Bob's is around 10,000.

YOU PUT WHAT ON THAT SANDWICH?

Where can you find French fries that come on top, instead of on the side, of a sandwich?

Slap a few slices of hearty deli meat and cheese, savory coleslaw, tomatoes, and a handful of French fries between two thickly sliced pieces of fresh Italian bread, and you've got yourself a Pittsburgh Sandwich, which is what folks outside of the area generally tend to call it. But for Pittsburghers, it will always be a Primanti Bros. sandwich. This no-frills style of meal is ideal for breakfast, lunch, and dinner or at two in the morning if you've been out hitting the Pittsburgh bars.

Stemming from a brilliant idea for feeding truckers who came into the Strip District during the Depression, Joe Primanti would make sandwiches wrapped in paper and sell them from a cart. Years later, Joe's cousin came up with another brilliant idea, to pile fried potatoes on the top, and the rest is delicious history.

Primanti Bros., once just a local restaurant in the city proper, has now expanded to include spots in Indiana, West Virginia, and Ohio, but it's the original location on the corner of 18th and Smallman Streets in the Strip that offers true tradition and quirky painted murals of city celebrities such as Christina Aguilera and Fred Rogers.

These days, the menu has expanded to include fish and even pierogi sandwiches, so feel free to order whatever strikes your

Limited edition sandwiches have included a ham, bacon, and kielbasa in honor of the Pittsburgh Penguins' HBK line, Carl Hagelin, Nick Bonino, and Phil Kessel.

For Pittsburghers, fries and slaw on a sandwich is as common as pb&j. Photo credit: Steven Locke

PRIMANTI BROS.

WHAT Famous sandwiches topped with French fries and slaw

WHERE 46 18th St.

COST Sandwich prices start at around $7.

PRO TIP The restaurant is super popular, so if you don't want to wait for a table, try visiting during off-peak hours.

primantibros.com

fancy—just don't ask for fries on the side. And the sandwiches are not for the culinary faint of heart, either. Massive in size, and pretty messy, the thin paper that they arrive at your table on (similar to the paper they were originally wrapped in) is great for cleaning up rogue slaw and fries.

BEST CAKE IN AMERICA

Where can you sample one of the best cakes in America?

What do you get when you put thick homemade custard cream between two fluffy layers of buttery vanilla cake, frost it with buttercream, and top the already-delicious concoction with sugared almonds? The Best Cake in America, of course!

Prantl's Bakery in Shadyside was given the accolade by the *Huffington Post* in 2018 and for very good reason. In addition to this prestigious title, the bakery has been deemed worthy of even more awards for its Burnt Almond Torte, which have included Best Wedding Cakes and Best Cake in Pennsylvania.

But how did the famous confection come to Pittsburgh? The cake was taste-tested by bakery owner Henry Prantl in 1969 during a trip to California. Due to an almond surplus in the state, he and fellow bakers were encouraged to create recipes using almonds to increase the nut's sales. Each baker tried to outshine the others, and Prantl was happy to test their creations. He then invented his own variation of their recipes, and, after a few test runs, the rest is sweet history.

PRANTL'S BAKERY

WHAT The Best Cake in America

WHERE 5525 Walnut St.

COST Whole tortes start at around $21, but if you want just a taste ask for the two-bite version: a Toasted Almond Cup.

PRO TIP If you can't make it to Shadyside, no worries. Prantl's has another location in Market Square that also offers the famous torte.

https://prantlsbakery.com

Cleveland-based Platform Beer Co. collaborated with Prantl's in 2019 to create a Burnt Almond Torte blond ale.

The best cake in America—Burnt Almond Torte from Prantl's. Photo credit: Steven Locke

But, apart from its ingredients, what makes it so special? It's the combination of the three textures (fluffy, creamy, and crunchy) that reward your mouth with each bite. Of course, there are versions of the Burnt Almond Torte around town at other bakeries, but it's Prantl's torte that established the tradition.

MOSTLY CLOUDY WITH A CHANCE OF MORE CLOUDS

How does Pittsburgh "undershine" Seattle with regard to weather conditions?

When you think of cities in the United States where the people don't see clear blue skies for weeks at a time, Seattle and Anchorage probably make the top of your short list. And while they are both actually in the top 10, it turns out that Pittsburgh trumps them all when it comes to cloud cover, holding the dubious distinction of No. 1 Cloudiest City in America.

When measuring cloudiest cities, we need to look at the duration of sunshine in a particular location. So, by default, the cloudiest cities in the United States—and the world, for that matter—offer the least amount of sunshine per year. While it may seem contradictory, it's similar to the concept that cold is essentially a lack of heat.

For 77 percent of the year, Pittsburgh is covered in clouds, meaning that Pittsburghers only see the beautiful sunshine bounce off the golden-colored bridges and make the rivers sparkle for a mere 2,021 hours every 365 days. And, if you were curious about which months get the least amount of sun, November through January only experience 60 hours of sunshine, tops.

So, where does Pittsburgh rank for cloudy days on our side of the globe? It ranks as the sixth cloudiest city in Central

Pittsburgh photographer Dave DiCello has shot beautiful photos from Mt. Washington of the Pittsburgh skyline featuring low-lying fog, which he calls "City in the Clouds" images.

Just because it's cloudy 77 percent of the time, it doesn't make the Pittsburgh skyline any less beautiful. Photo credit: Steven Locke

CLOUDY PITTSBURGH DAYS

WHAT The #1 cloudiest city in America

WHERE All across Pittsburgh

COST Free to view

PRO TIP Even though Pittsburgh is covered in clouds for over three-quarters of the year, it's no excuse not to wear sunscreen.

and North America. As for a worldwide ranking, Tórshavn across Denmark's Faroe Islands wins the award for Cloudiest Place in the World.

So, if you're planning on heading up to Mount Washington to get a photo of a sunny Pittsburgh skyline, you may have to do some serious planning—and hope the Pittsburgh meteorologists are on point with their accuracy for the day.

HEAVEN, I'M IN (BICYCLE) HEAVEN

Where can you find one of the most well-known movie bikes from the 1980s?

In the mid-1990s, Craig Morrow found a beat up, old bicycle in a bunch of junk. And all it took was that particular bike to inspire Mr. Morrow. He started finding and repairing old bikes, keeping well over 3,000 in garages all around the Bellevue area of town. Eventually, he and his wife turned his passion into the world's largest bicycle museum and shop, Bicycle Heaven. Officially established in 2011, the shop offers folks a chance to get bike repairs and offers trade-ins for both new and old bicycles.

But what is unique about Bicycle Heaven is the fact that these days, it has more than 6,000 bikes under one roof, including some truly impressive pieces. For '80s cult classic movie fans, the top of the list would be the decked-out and highly memorable red-and-white bike from *Pee Wee's Big Adventure* that took Pee Wee Herman on a country-wide hunt for his prized mode of transportation.

BICYCLE HEAVEN

WHAT A bike shop/famous bicycle collection

WHERE 1800 Preble Ave.

COST Free to browse, bicycles vary in price

PRO TIP If you want to see Pittsburgh via two wheels, Bicycle Heaven rents them as well.

www.bicycleheaven.org

Bicycle Heaven has more than 10,000 parts in stock to keep its collection up to par.

If you're a fan of '80s cult classic movies, you'll know to what lengths Pee Wee Herman went to get his bicycle back. Photo credit: www.flickr.com/photos/the-spoo

If you're all about themes with a musical twist, look no further: bicycle tributes to both the Beatles and Elvis Presley can be viewed in the museum. And if it's rare two-wheelers you dig, you'll find not one, but 17 Bowden Spacelanders (the first fiberglass bicycle ever made), with only 30 known to still be around.

CATSUP TO PITTSBURGH

How did the No. 1 selling brand of ketchup get its start from a Chinese recipe?

For business owner Henry John Heinz, 1869 was a big year. Sure, he'd already had several bottled condiments doing well on store shelves, but for Pittsburghers, that was the year the businessman began selling condiments in glass bottles.

Commonly known as H. J. Heinz, he got his start from selling products from a wheelbarrow, ended up going to jail for bankruptcy for a time, and started fresh in 1876, the same year that Heinz ketchup (then named catsup) became the sandwich-sauce rage.

Created as a better version of a 1,000-year old Chinese fish sauce, the sweet, tangy condiment is still the No. 1 selling brand. By the time 1907 rolled around, Heinz was selling 13 million bottles of ketchup to Pittsburghers and sandwich lovers around the world. H. J. Heinz can also be considered a forward thinker in regard to bottled sauces: since 1906, his version of ketchup has been produced without preservatives.

Today, Heinz Ketchup comes in several styles to adorn food of the health conscious as well. There are styles with both no salt and no sugar added, organic, and blended vegetables. But some of the most memorables styles are the ones that debuted in the year 2000: the company got creative and made ketchup in purple, pink, blue, teal, and orange. A cool craze for a minute, the colors lost selling steam and left the store shelves.

Sadly, the product is no longer made in Pittsburgh; instead, our factory produces baby food and instant soup for store

---

In the year 2000, Heinz created a green ketchup which was sold in a plastic squirt bottle.

In Pittsburgh, is there really another brand? Photo credit: www.flickr.com/photos/ jeepersmedia/

shelves. So, while that famous sauce in its signature octagonal glass bottle is no longer technically from Pittsburgh, the roots of building a better mousetrap, er, Chinese fish sauce, are all ours.

HEINZ KETCHUP

WHAT #1 selling brand of ketchup

WHERE In just about every Pittsburgh grocery store

COST $3

PRO TIP You'd be hard-pressed to not find Heinz Ketchup in a Pittsburgh restaurant, but if you do, consider it a rarity!

31 CULTURAL CELEBRATIONS UNDER ONE ROOF

How can you see winter celebrations from around the world under one college roof?

In Oakland, look to the upper skyline to get an easy view of the Cathedral of Learning. But delve a little deeper inside the University of Pittsburgh's skyscraper, and you'll find so much more. In fact, 31 classrooms, commonly known as its Nationality Rooms, provide places for classes as well as education about countries from all over the world.

Created and designed to represent the ethnic groups who call Allegheny County their home, each of the Nationality Rooms was specifically designed by the represented country's committee, which plans and pays for every detail down to the door's handle.

Of the 31 rooms on the first and third floors, 29 are used for classes and can literally be walked into and toured when class is not in session. The rooms are fun to visit at any time of year, but they are really amped up during the winter holidays with beautiful decorations to celebrate national, religious, and even traditional holidays, compliments of their respective ethnic committees.

NATIONALITY ROOMS AT THE CATHEDRAL OF LEARNING

WHAT Uniquely themed school rooms at the University of Pittsburgh

WHERE 4200 Fifth Ave.

COST Self-guided viewing is free. Tours: Adults $4, Children 6-18 $2.

PRO TIP Seeing the Nationality Rooms decked out in their holiday splendor is a must!

www.nationalityrooms.pitt.edu

The ornate Austrian Room, one of 31 at the Cathedral of Learning in Oakland. Photo credit: Steven Locke

In 2019, the Philippine Room was the most recent to be dedicated while the Korean Room was its predecessor in 2015. Why so much time in between? Many rooms can take up to 10 years and $750,000 to complete due to the need for raising funds for construction.

The Cathedral of Learning is the only skyscraper in Oakland.

THE BEST 360-DEGREE VIEW OF THE CITY—BUT ONLY ONCE A YEAR

Where can you go once a year to see a 360-degree view of the city?

In Pittsburgh, the tallest building in the downtown area since 1967 has been the US Steel Tower. Affectionately referred to as the Steel Building by the locals, the skyscraper comes in at 841 feet with the second tallest skyscraper (BNY Mellon Building) well under 100 feet shorter at 725 feet in height. And since it lacks peaks, it also holds the distinction of being the tallest building in the world with a completely flat roof.

With its ideal location in the center part of the Golden Triangle area of downtown, there's no doubt that the view from the roof is incredible, even on cloudy Pittsburgh days. Until 2001, guests could get almost the same view from Top of the Triangle, a swanky restaurant on the 62nd floor.

Sadly, these days, apart from employees doing security checks, that view is available to visitors only a couple of times a year. But, if you can't get up to the top, the building's architecture is pretty stunning too. A triangular shape with indented corners, the style was created to emulate the shape of the Golden Triangle. And if you can't get to the city to see it in person, you can catch glimpses of it everywhere from the movies *Dogma* and *The Dark Knight Rises* to the popular video game *Fallout 3*.

US Steel Tower is the fifth-tallest building in Pennsylvania and the 200th-tallest in the world.

A once-in-a-lifetime (or a year!) view of Pittsburgh via US Steel Tower observation deck. Photo credit: Steven Locke

On very special occasions, the US Steel Tower, in partnership with the Downtown Pittsburgh Partnership, opens its roof to guests for a few hours on one night only during the VIP Blast Party on Light-Up Night, the night when the city turns on its Christmas lights to officially kick off the holiday season. Trust me, that view is worth the ticket price.

OBSERVATION DECK AT US STEEL TOWER

WHAT A 360-degree view of the city

WHERE US Steel Tower at the corner of Grant Street and Fifth Avenue

COST VIP Blast Party admission (prices vary)

PRO TIP The view from the observation deck is very popular during the party, and it gets pretty windy so dress very warmly.

downtownpittsburghholidays.com/blast

PICKLED TINK

How can a tiny pin show love for Pittsburgh's food scene?

Beginning in the 1800s, if you took a tour of the H. J. Heinz Factory in Pittsburgh, your reward for a tour well given was a teeny pickle pin to wear on your hat, shirt, or coat. While many of us know H. J. Heinz as the creator of the popular condiment, ketchup, one of the first products he ever bottled was pickles. To add more to the cool story, Heinz had another delicious first: he was the originator of sweet pickles.

PICKLESBURGH

WHAT A festival celebrating all-things pickled

WHERE Roberto Clemente Bridge, downtown Pittsburgh

COST Free, prices vary for food and souvenirs

PRO TIP Bring your appetite and food curiosity, and be ready to try some unusual dishes.

www.picklesburgh.com

For that Pittsburgh pickle pride, it comes as no surprise that for one weekend every year, the city transforms its riverfront area into a fun festival called Picklesburgh featuring all things pickled. Sure, there are plenty of sweet and savory pickle dishes (including some bizarre dishes like ice cream and candy), but the festival is also a tribute to the pickling process itself.

The city's culinary celebration is designed to delight the palates of pickle lovers with all things pickled, but it's definitely the atmosphere on and around the Roberto Clemente Bridge (one of the three Sister Bridges connecting the Golden Triangle area to the North Shore) that's addictively fun. You'll find everything from pickle merchandise (including those teeny pickle pins) to a giant Heinz pickle balloon detailed enough to make you think it belongs in one of the Macy's parades in Manhattan.

Even if you're not a fan of pickles or the pickling process, the event is truly a fun time to hang with local sour-flavor

Pickled everything at the popular Picklesburgh, even a giant pickle balloon!
Photo credit: www.flickr.com/photos/namoscato

lovers and learn a thing or two about the process. Plus, you can always have an "I dare you" contest to try one of the many free samples of specialty foods created from the adoration.

In 2019, Kraft Heinz gave out golden special-edition pickle pins at Picklesburgh to celebrate its 150-year anniversary.

DECONSECRATED BREW

How did a deconsecrated church become a popular spot for craft brew lovers?

For 91 years, St. John the Baptist Roman Catholic Church in Lawrenceville served as a community spiritual sanctuary. Sadly, a decline in parishioners and funds to keep it running caused the church to close its doors on August 6, 1993. It was then deconsecrated to allow for the building and its property to be sold for nonreligious purposes.

Two days short of three years later, The Church Brew Works opened its doors and offered locals a beautifully restored building and some good brew to go with it. Paying homage to the church, its handcrafted brews are given creative religious names such as Pipe Organ Pale Ale and Pious Monk Dunkel, two of its flagship brews. The brew pub gets seasonally creative as well and offers its beer lovers everything from sours to stouts.

Repurposing items from St. John the Baptist, pieces such as the original church pews were cut down and turned into seats to accommodate diners. Discovered under old plywood, its Douglas fir wood floors were restored to their original, beautiful glory. Even one of the confessionals was put to good use: it became the home for The Church Brew Works merchandise behind the bar.

If you were thinking that it serves the usual pub food, you're in for a surprise: its menu includes everything from

---

In 2012, The Church Brew Works was named Large Brewpub of the Year by the Great American Beer Festival.

The Church Brew Works, a sacred space turned brewery and restaurant. Photo credit: Steven Locke

lobster mac n' cheese to Kobe Beef sandwiches. With the fun menu, especially if you're a beer lover, you'll definitely want to try a couple of its award-winning beers—the company has more than 25 medals to date.

THE CHURCH BREW WORKS

WHAT A former church turned restaurant and brew pub

WHERE 525 Liberty Ave.

COST Free to enter, menu prices vary. Must be 21+ to enjoy its brew selections.

PRO TIP The Church Brew Works is a super popular Pittsburgh restaurant, so consider making reservations ahead of time.

https://churchbrew.com

OLD-SCHOOL OYSTERS

How is it that the oldest restaurant in Pittsburgh is still a thriving business for seafood lovers?

If you want to dine in the oldest restaurant in town, look no further than the Original Oyster House in the Market Square area of downtown. When the restaurant opened its doors to the public in 1870, oysters were a mere penny a piece, and beer was only 10 cents a glass! These days, you'll be hard-pressed to find anyone who can remember such low prices, but it's always fun to reminisce about the cost of living in Pittsburgh during the 19th-century.

And while its age is something to be admired, its current owner's story is just as admirable. When Louis Grippo was a teenager, he was booted out of the restaurant, so he made a vow to himself to return one day and purchase it. Although it took many years for his dream to come true, he became the owner in 1970—a century after it opened its doors for the first time.

These days, the breaded oysters and famous fish sandwiches are menu staples. Also a big draw is the authentic, old-school feel of the place: filmmakers of all genres have used the Original Oyster House as a backdrop for more than 25 movies.

ORIGINAL OYSTER HOUSE

WHAT Oldest restaurant in Pittsburgh

WHERE 20 Market Square

COST Menu prices vary

PRO TIP If you dig oysters, this is your go-to place in Pittsburgh.

www.originaloysterhouse
pittsburgh.com

Original Oyster House calls one of its fish sandwiches the Cod Father.

Old-time cool, especially the oysters, at Original Oyster House in Market Square. Photo credit: Steven Locke

PITTSBURGHESE

How did Pittsburgh's dialect become a symbol of the melding of its immigrants?

Jeet your butterbread yet? Naw, d'jew? Hey, did you see all of those brown-calered jaggers on the side of the slippy road near my nebby neighbors? Before I leave, I gotta redd up, sweep the carpet, and arn before I look for my gumbands. If you think you've just read a foreign language, you didn't. Actually, it's only Yinzer! Did yinz get to Da Burgh last week? We got dahntahn for a sammich and a chitchat but had to get home to fix our spicket so we could worsh our car.

If you're a visitor to Pittsburgh, talk to a few of its born-and-raised residents, and you may hear a unique-to-the-area dialect containing words that you have no idea what they mean. This fun pronunciation of words (and the words themselves) is referred to as Yinzer or Pittsburghese. And while locals may not even notice the way they speak, in 2014, the accent was dubbed America's Ugliest by Gawker.com.

The dialect's uniqueness comes from locals engaging with immigrants starting in the 19th and 20th centuries. Scottish, Irish, German, Polish, Croatian, and African immigrants all added their unique ways of speaking to Pittsburgh's local dialect, and voila! Pittsburghese was born. So, the Scots-Irish can be credited for the terms "redd up" instead of clean up and "nebby" instead of nosy and the Germans are responsible for the shortened "butterbread" instead of buttered bread.

Even more, local radio stations such as WDVE have given their listeners some good humor with skits filled with local

---

"Yinzer" was the name given to Pittsburgh blue-collar workers and their heavy local accent.

A T-shirt with all the Pittsburghese at PGH Sports in the Strip District. Photo credit: Steven Locke

yinzers talking about a day in the life. And, if you really want a blast from the musical past, give a listen to the fight song, "Here We Go!" for a deadpan yinzer singing style and tribute to the Pittsburgh Steelers all at once.

BAR CITY?

How did Pittsburgh gain the title of the City with the Most Bars?

If you want to relax with a beer or hang out with some locals on the weekend, Pittsburgh's the right city to visit because of the number of local brew pubs popping up all over town. In fact, Pittsburgh was given the title of City with the Most Bars per Capita in the United States. With just under 12 bars per 10,000 residents (11.8 bars, to be exact), there is no shortage of places to grab a drink.

So, just where are all of these bars? Apart from a few saturated spots, such as the South Side, downtown in and around the Cultural District, and Bloomfield, they're local hangouts with some pretty cool history: new ones with hip vibes (the 2015 movie *Fathers and Daughters* with Russell Crowe has scenes in Butcher and the Rye) or classy cocktail bars with a fun take on traditional drinks can be found all over the city. If you really want an authentic vibe, head to one of its dozens of dive bars for a cheap beer and laid-back atmosphere.

Happily, if you have a case of the munchies after spending time hanging out at a local watering hole, no worries there, either: Pittsburgh comes in second for pizza shops per capita, with 9.9 pizzerias per 10,000 people.

PITTSBURGH BARS

WHAT The city with the most bars per capita

WHERE All around the city

COST Most don't have a cover charge, menu prices vary

PRO TIP If you really want to cover a lot of bars in one night, the South Side is the place to go.

Handcrafted soda at Butcher and the Rye. Who says you have to drink liquor in a hip, Pittsburgh bar, right? Photo credit: Steven Locke

The famous Mawby's bar scenes in *Flashdance* were actually filmed in a Los Angeles bar.

20 YEARS OF "H" CONTENTION

Why did Pittsburgh's "h" get dropped and then added again?

When General John Forbes sent a letter to William Pitt the Elder, 1st Earl of Chatham, on November 27, 1758, stating that the area of Fort Duquesne was named "Pittsbourgh," it was the first official reference known. But, compliments of a printing error, it was spelled "Pittsburg."

Roughly 103 years later, 13 principles were adopted by the US Board on Geographic Names, including dropping the "h" on cities where the name ended in "burgh." The new spelling didn't go over well for some residents, and businesses such as the University of Pittsburgh flat-out refused to change. Additionally, a local newspaper, the *Pittsburgh Gazette*, downright refused to change the spelling in its pages, continuing to print the h.

As a result of pressure put on the Board to revert the spelling back to Pittsburgh, in 1911, the "h" was restored. Currently, there are a few cities named after Pittsburgh (in California and Kansas, among others) that spell the name without an "h," but it's the fight to keep it in the name that makes for a fun tale to tell.

If you look hard enough, you'll find a few remaining references to "Pittsburg" around the city on road signs,

---

The most collectible baseball card in the world with a value of over $3 million, the 1909–1911 Honus Wagner Pirates baseball card has a photo of the athlete in uniform with "Pittsburg" written on it.

Pittsburgh without the "h" in Chester, West Virginia. Photo credit: Karyn Locke

THE LACK OF THE PITTSBURGH "H"

WHAT The evolution of spelling the city's name

WHERE Downtown's Union Station at Grant St. and Liberty Ave.

COST Free to view

PRO TIP Look inside the station's rotunda for the "Pittsburg" reference.

inside downtown's Union Station, on the train station on the corner of Grant Street and Liberty Avenue, and in the small town of Chester, WV. Recently, I spotted a street sign in the city of Canton, Ohio, named Pittsburg Avenue too. So, now it's fun to look for the missing "h" and giggle about Pittsburgh's fervor for keeping it intact.

DEFY GRAVITY IN NORTH PARK

Where can you defy gravity by driving?

At one specific stop sign on McKinney Road in North Park, you can come to a complete stop, put your car in neutral, and then put your foot on the brake. Checking for traffic first, of course, take your foot off the brake, and your vehicle will astound you as it seems to defy gravity by slowly rolling back up the hill you just came down.

This gravity-defying spot, known as a Gravity Hill or Magnetic Hill, delights North Park visitors who want to use their cars for a good jaw-dropping driving event or a way to fascinate the kids.

I know we all like to believe in magic, but truthfully the cool stunt is merely an optical illusion compliments of the way the land features surround the road. So, what looks like a small downward slope is actually the opposite of what your eyes and brain are telling you.

Don't think that the illusion works only on vehicles, either. On no-traffic days, folks can get really creative with their tests by using bowling balls or other small round objects. If you really want to try a fun test, pour some water at the stop sign and watch where it flows.

GRAVITY HILL

WHAT An optical illusion making you feel like you're rolling uphill

WHERE 461 McKinney Rd., Wexford

COST Free

PRO TIP If you want to give Gravity Hill a go, make sure traffic is light and be cautious.

There are more than 115 Gravity Hills all over the world.

It might not look like much in photos, but Gravity Hill is definitely worth trying in person if you're in the North Park area. Photo credit: Steven Locke

While there are hundreds of these gravity hills all over the world, North Park's is the only one in the Pittsburgh area. The next-closest one is located in the Laurel Caverns area of the Laurel Highlands.

GO STEAGLES!

How is it that two NFL football teams combined names for one season?

In 1943, it was not uncommon for football players to be drafted into the military due to World War II. As a result, several teams—the Pittsburgh Steelers and the Philadelphia Eagles, included—had very short player rosters. So, combining two teams into one made perfect sense, both financially and to maintain player numbers.

That year, the Phil-Pitt Combine team played both their first and last season with a total of 25 players. What makes the team even more unusual is the fact that several of the players had ailments that would normally have prohibited them from participating in an NFL game: sleepwalking, diabetes, perforated eardrums, and even high blood pressure. Top it off with the men having full-time jobs, and you can definitely see what made this season unique.

Taking parts of two separate words to make an entirely new word (a.k.a., a portmanteau) is not unusual these days. But, when an editor from Pittsburgh combined the Steelers and Eagles to make the name "Steagles," it was well-received by the press and fans. The team didn't go on to win a championship title that year, but the memory of the Steagles and their green and white jerseys will go down in NFL history.

STEAGLES

WHAT The combination of Pittsburgh Steelers and Philadelphia Eagles for a single season

WHERE In the memories of fans

COST Free to reminisce

PRO TIP If you like the idea of showing love for the Steagles, check online for an affordable T-shirt.

The Steagles may have been a one-season-only football team, but memorabilia in honor of the team can still be found—like this notebook. Photo credit: Steven Locke

The Steagles split its home games between Forbes Field in Pittsburgh and Shibe Park in Philly.

IMMACULATE DOMINATION

How did one brilliant football catch steamroll an NFL team to victory?

If you love watching American football game replays, hands down one of the best and one of the most controversial was the "Immaculate Reception" during a Pittsburgh Steelers vs. Oakland Raiders game. Not only did it clinch a first-ever playoff win for the Pittsburgh Steelers in 1972, but it helped the team to steamroll their winning streak into four Super Bowl victories by the time the 1980s arrived.

Making a pun from "Immaculate Conception," a phrase used in Catholic doctrine, the Immaculate Reception occurred as a result of the efforts of four players on the field. With the Pittsburgh Steelers down in the fourth quarter 7-6, and with only 30 seconds left in the game, quarterback Terry Bradshaw threw the ball to the Raiders' 35-yard line toward teammate and halfback John Fuqua. Jack Tatum, an Oakland Raiders safety, collided with Fuqua causing the ball to sail backwards. Right before the football hit the ground, Steelers fullback Franco Harris grabbed the ball and ran for a touchdown, making the game's final score 13-7.

The next week, the Steelers lost the AFC Championship game to the Miami Dolphins, but that didn't deter the team from being one of two with the most Super Bowl wins—tied with the New England Patriots with six each. As for the Immaculate Reception, a monument marking the exact spot it occurred can be found on the North Shore.

IMMACULATE RECEPTION

WHAT A game-changing play for the Pittsburgh Steelers

WHERE Monument can be found on the North Shore between PNC Park and Heinz Field

COST Free

PRO TIP Make sure to look on the ground for the exact spot where Franco Harris caught the game-winning football.

You can literally put your foot where the Immaculate Reception occurred on the North Shore. Photo credit: Steven Locke

Running Back Franco Harris played for the Pittsburgh Steelers for 12 seasons and has four Super Bowl Championship wins under his belt.

SELDOM-SEEN BEAUTY

Where in Pittsburgh can you visit a place that has a rundown beauty?

When you're up at the top of Mt. Washington looking across the Monongahela River to the Golden Triangle area of the city, it might seem hard to believe that there's a more than 90-acre green space at the foot of the mountain called Seldom Seen. Located along Saw Mill Run Boulevard in Beechview, a visit to Seldom Seen feels like a step back in time as soon as you head through its gate.

Once a teeny village annexed by the city in the mid-1920s, there were still a few residents up until the 1960s. Sadly, as the people moved out, the trash moved in, and it then turned into an illegal dumping site where folks threw their garbage, old tires, and anything they couldn't fit into a trash can.

But there was a happy ending for this area with a fairy-tale name. These days, Seldom Seen has been beautifully reclaimed by nature. The location offers visitors a chance to spy the scattered remains of the 12-house German village and to imagine what it looked like back in the day. But what about the dump site? Compliments of some truly kind and selfless folks, the woods and water areas stay clean as a result of voluntary cleanup sessions a couple of times a year.

SELDOM SEEN

WHAT A beautiful green space that was once a German village

WHERE Watkins Rd. Trail

COST Free

PRO TIP It's best to visit Seldom Seen during warmer weather as the greenery makes the area look even more otherworldly.

www.facebook.com/pages/Beechview-Seldom-Seen-Greenway/696251320412653

Seldom Seen is located in Beechview—also the home of Canton Avenue, the steepest street in America.

A place called Seldom Seen is now home to a gorgeous outdoor space. Photo credit: Steven Locke

TUNNELS OF FUN FACTS

What's the BIG deal about Pittsburgh tunnels?

There's always a running joke about Pittsburgh tunnels that either involves the vehicle backups when trying to get in or out or the fact that each is a single lane and you have only a couple of seconds to merge into a new lane, to get where you need to be. Apart from the snarky, but truthful, humor, the facts surrounding Pittsburgh's Liberty, Squirrel Hill, Fort Pitt, and Stowe tunnels (the oldest of the four sets) are fascinating, to say the least.

While going through the Liberty Tunnels at full speed is a dream, consider this fun fact: when built in 1924, the tunnels actually had plenty of horse and buggy traffic. And, until a ventilation system was installed, horses and their owners would often pass out due to the high levels of carbon monoxide. Eventually in the 1940s horses were banned.

As for the tunnel facade architecture, it's pretty fascinating too. Built in 1946, the Squirrel Hill Tunnels were built with a smaller economy in mind, so you'll see affordable sandstone. But, when it comes to the Fort Pitt Tunnels, it's all about beautiful marble exteriors, showcasing the city's more affluent times in the 1960s.

PITTSBURGH TUNNELS

WHAT Fun facts

WHERE Around the city

COST Free, apart from the time it takes due to backed-up traffic

PRO TIP If you're only going through the tunnels for nostalgia, drive through during nonpeak traffic times of the day.

Up until 2015, Fort Pitt Tunnels had a flat ceiling. It was removed due to its poor condition and never replaced.

The history behind the Pittsburgh tunnels is almost as cool as driving through them. Photo credit: Pixabay

What about the sheer size of the tunnels? If lined up end to end, the tunnels would span 14,228 feet! As for the longest of the four sets, it's the Liberty Tunnels coming in at 5,889 feet in length. Keeping up with Liberty Tunnel facts, there was even an "inebriation holding cell" on the city side that would house drunkards from the downtown area until they sobered up the next morning.

WHERE TROLLEYS GO TO DIE

Where can you see old trolleys left to be reclaimed by nature?

When you think of the 20th century and current mechanized transportation, you can't help but remember the trolley, an efficient way for folks to get around larger cities. After all, hundreds of miles of trolley tracks lined the streets of Pittsburgh for nearly a century from the late 1800s to the early 1980s, first starting with horse-drawn cars and eventually becoming all-electric versions.

Eventually trolleys were completely replaced with light rail cars and buses in Pittsburgh as trolley transportation had become obsolete. Happily, however, if you want to take a peek at a few of the old cars, there's a place just outside of Pittsburgh for that.

If you enjoy the beauty of abandoned history, there is a cemetery for more than 40 trolleys located southeast of Pittsburgh in Windber. Affectionately referred to as the Trolley Graveyard, dilapidated and rusting trolley cars are slowly becoming part of the woods that surround them.

But how did they get to such a remote location? Ed Metka, retired civil engineer, started acquiring the trolleys in 1986 and

The first electric streetcars for commercial use were used in Cleveland, Ohio, in 1884.

A beautiful trolley being reclaimed by nature at the Trolley Graveyard of Windber. Photo credit: www.flickr.com/photos/55229469@N07/

moved his collection via flatbed truck to Windber in 1992 when the number outgrew his storage space in Maryland. He's still all about restoring the finer cars and parts out many of the others when the few still-running trolley cars need repair and parts have become impossible to find.

DO YOU WANT THREE SCOOPS OR FOUR?

Where can you find the birthplace of the banana split?

People all over America—and the world, for that matter—have enjoyed ice cream as a special treat and way to cool off on hot summer days. But it was just east of Pittsburgh where the ice cream sundae on steroids—the banana split—was born, turning eating ice cream sundaes into an American pastime.

In the late 1800s in Latrobe (the hometown of Mister Rogers), bananas were readily available to Americans. In 1904, pharmacist David Strickler, trying to increase ice cream sales at the Tassell Pharmacy and at the request of a Saint Vincent College student looking for something different, cut a banana in half lengthwise; added a scoop each of vanilla, chocolate, and strawberry ice cream; and put some whipped cream on top with a cherry—and just like that, the banana split was born.

While this take on an ice cream sundae wasn't an immediate hit, popularity did begin to grow when the

The World's Longest Banana Split was created in Innisfail, Australia, in 2017 and used 40,000 bananas.

A giant banana split tribute in downtown Latrobe, Pennsylvania. Photo credit: Karyn Locke

college students took the sundae idea back to their respective hometowns. As for the oval-shaped dish that a banana split traditionally comes in, Strickler gets the credit for that too.

To keep the banana split love going, Latrobe holds its annual Great American Banana Split Celebration on August 25th, the same day that the rest of America celebrates National Banana Split Day.

DON'T THROW OUT MY STUFF!

How did a popular modern artist turn his everyday life into a time capsule?

Hometown hero and uber-popular modern art creator Andy Warhol had a thing for keeping everything, and I mean everything. From food scraps to a mummified human foot, Warhol kept these accumulations in daily "time capsules" for about 13 years. A total of 610 time-capsule pieces, cardboard boxes, filing cabinets, and one large trunk offered a unique glimpse into the artist's daily life over a four-decade period.

For years, the time capsules just sat around waiting for someone to explore their contents. So, it makes absolute sense that curators at the Andy Warhol Museum in Pittsburgh's North Shore area and the largest museum in North America dedicated to a single artist, would take on the task of meticulously identifying and logging the contents of each to gain insight into the artist's life. At any given time at the museum, one of Warhol's capsule contents is always on display on the third floor. On average, each capsule contains around 250 items ranging from the mundane (daily newspapers and fashion magazine) to the extraordinary (metal dental molds and Truman Capote interview transcripts) to everything in between. Of course, these capsules were meant to be art pieces in Warhol's eyes and are treated as such by the openers.

But there's far more to look at than just his time capsules when you visit. You'll find thousands of his art pieces, including

Time Capsules was Andy Warhol's largest collecting project.

Andy Warhol loved painting boxes—and adding bits and pieces of his daily life into them too. Photo credit: Steven Locke

ANDY WARHOL MUSEUM

WHAT A museum dedicated to Warhol and his daily collections

WHERE 117 Sandusky St.

COST $20; Students, Children 3-18, and Seniors (65+) $10; Children 0-2 and Members free

PRO TIP Half-price for admission on Fridays from 5—10 p.m.

www.warhol.org

900 paintings (one made with his own urine!), 77 sculptures, thousands of drawings and illustrations, and 350 films. Add in large and small items he'd collected over the years (he loved daily shopping sprees), such as the taxidermy lion and Great Dane, and it's a seven-floor tribute to a man passionate for pop culture.

EAST OF TINSELTOWN

How did Pittsburgh become a prominent filmmaking city?

For big cities on the coasts, such as New York or Los Angeles, filming a movie on location is a common occurrence. But for Middle America, it's a much rarer occasion—except in Pittsburgh. To give props to Pittsburgh's booming filming scene, the city was nicknamed the Tinseltown of the East by CNN in the early 2010s due to the frequency of both movie and TV show filming there.

Films have been made in Pittsburgh since 1914, beginning with *The Perils of Pauline*, but lately, the city has seen a massive increase in the number of films and shows thanks to a tax incentive offered to filmmakers by the city. Consequently, blockbuster films from *The Dark Knight Rises* and *Silence of the Lambs* to cult classics such as *Dogma* and *Night of the Living Dead* have only helped to lock in Pittsburgh's new title.

More recently, films such as *A Beautiful Day in the Neighborhood* and *Where'd You Go, Bernadette* (with a couple of quick glimpses of yours truly during the office scenes) have truly put the city on the movie map.

TINSELTOWN OF THE EAST

WHAT Pittsburgh's booming film scene

WHERE Locations around Pittsburgh

COST Free

PRO TIP Compile a list of your favorite movies filmed in Pittsburgh, and create your own walking/driving tour.

www.pghfilm.org/screening-room/pittsburgh-filmography

At least 275 movies have been shot in and around Pittsburgh.

A tribute to one of Pittsburgh's city-made movies, Night of the Living Dead. *Photo credit: Karyn Locke*

But why is Pittsburgh so ideal for filming movies of all genres? Apart from a desert or beach backdrop, the city has just about every other look you could want, including authentic 1970s and 1980s looks in some of its boroughs, rundown steel mills, and modern cityscapes.

"LADIES AND GENTLEMEN, I GIVE YOU . . . THE SKY!"

Where can you see a clear view of the Pittsburgh sky while still indoors?

Divided into eight individual sections, the Civic Arena in Pittsburgh's downtown area at the top of the Golden Triangle was built in 1961 for $22 million. Built as the first major-league sports venue with a retractable dome, it was home to the Pittsburgh Penguins NHL team from 1967 to 2010. Its first-ever event was the traveling Ice Capades on September 17, 1961, and during the time it was in full swing, it offered large shows from rock concerts to the circus to Elvis Presley's final New Year's Eve concert in 1976.

It was during a live performance of *The Carol Burnett Show* on July 4, 1962, that the dome opened for the first time to the delight of fans. It took a lengthy two-and-a-half minutes to fold eight separate sections into two, and Ms. Burnett, always ready with a good one-liner, exclaimed, "Ladies and Gentlemen, I give you . . . the sky!" when it fully opened.

The venue kept its name until 1999 when it was renamed Mellon Arena, and the owners stopped opening the dome in 2001 due to large repair and operating costs. The Arena officially closed its doors on June 26, 2010, and these days, all that's left are the parking areas that surrounded it, now used for PPG Paints Arena parking.

If you want to see glimpses of the Civic Arena in film, check out the 1995 movie *Sudden Death* with Jean-Claude

Before it closed, Civic Arena's address was 66 Mario Lemieux Place.

The Civic Arena, home to countless shows and concerts through the '90s. Photo credit: www.flickr.com/photos/pquan

Van Damme (my parents were extras in it!), or 2001's *Rock Star* featuring Jennifer Aniston and Mark Wahlberg and the hilarious parking lot scene. And, if you're up for a good rom-com, *She's Out of My League* has a date scene with the Pittsburgh Penguins and the arena as the backdrop.

CIVIC ARENA

WHAT First major-league venue retractable dome

WHERE In our hearts. Its former location is across the street from PPG Paints Arena.

COST Free to reminisce

PRO TIP If you're a die-hard fan of the arena, you can still visit its former site.

FOUR-SEASON MINIATURE FUN

Where can you see tiny replicas of prominent Pittsburgh-region locations?

In 1919, in the town of Brookville, Pennsylvania, a man named Charles Bowdish created a holiday miniature village display on the second floor of his house to delight family and friends visiting and celebrating the season. Including Lionel Trains, the scene depicted intricately decorated mini models of buildings around his hometown. To keep the display fresh, each year he'd change the theme of the display, and each year more and more folks came to visit the detailed diorama.

As a result of a flood at the location where he kept the pieces stored when not on view and because his insurance company was unable to cover the crowds of people who regularly visited his miniature village, Bowdish offered his pieces to Buhl Planetarium and Institute, which opened the exhibit under the name The Great Christmastown Railroad on December 1, 1954. Renamed the Miniature Railroad & Village® in 1957, the miniature train display went to its current home at the Carnegie Science Center where the exhibit opened in 1992.

MINIATURE RAILROAD & VILLAGE®

WHAT Giant miniature train display filled with Western Pennsylvanian locations

WHERE Carnegie Science Center, 1 Allegheny Ave.

COST Adults $19.95, Seniors $14.95, Children 3-12 $11.95

PRO TIP Science Center admission includes the miniature railroad exhibit along with four floors of educational fun.

www.carnegiesciencecenter.org/exhibits/miniature-railroad

The latest addition to the Miniature Railroad & Village® at Carnegie Science Center: Kaufmann's Department Store. Photo credit: Karyn Locke

What makes the display so fascinating, especially for Pittsburghers, is the fact that it pays homage to 1880-1930-era Western Pennsylvania during all four seasons. In addition, each year before the official start of the winter holiday season, a new display piece is added to the collection. Popular miniatures include the Frank Lloyd Wright–designed house Fallingwater, Forbes Field, Kaufmann's Department Store and Clock, and *Mister Rogers' Neighborhood's* famous set house.

Fans in the Forbes Field stadium miniature are made from cotton swabs.

"MIST"ERIOUS PATH

Where can you take a walk through a creepy blue mist?

Whether or not you believe, or just want to believe, in paranormal occurrences, chances are you've heard a tale or two about locations where people met with tragic endings and their spirits remained behind. For Blue Mist Road in the McCandless area, there's not just one creepy story complete with spooky ambiance, there are several. If the mist isn't enough to cause you to make a beeline for a more urban, less desolate spot, a local legend claims that if ghost hunter wannabes honk the car horn three times (why is it always in threes?), the spirits of the dead will awaken to haunt them.

Almost every night at sundown, an eerie blue mist shrouds a section of Irwin Road (the real name of Blue Mist Road), and believers swear that it's due to the high paranormal activity that goes on in the area. The actual section in question is completely closed off, but folks somehow manage to hike and walk along the gravel path.

One of the most popular scary tales of Blue Mist Road features a set of cemetery headstones that almost "kiss" each other as there are supposed to be former lovers buried underneath them. Other stories offer creepy tales of a rabid dog, a witch house, and unusual lights.

BLUE MIST ROAD

WHAT A road that has eerie blue mist at night

WHERE Irwin Rd., Gibsonia

COST Free

PRO TIP Play it safe and visit with a friend, especially if you spook easily.

Shine your headlights on the blue mist for an even creepier ambiance.

Pretty views of Blue Mist Road are even prettier (if you think creepy's pretty) at night. Photo credit: Steven Locke

PUBLIC ART WITH FORESIGHT

Where can you see random tiles buried in street blacktop for no apparent reason?

In and around downtown Pittsburgh, especially if you're walking, you can see several prominent public art pieces. There are variations on dinosaurs, cool jazz musicians who are larger than life, and lighted alleyways that mimic twinkling stars overheard. But, the most curious pieces ever to make their way into the city require you to hunt and keep your eyes on the roads. What's even more curious is that no one really knows how they got there or who made them.

Toynbee Tiles (more than likely referring to 20th century British philosopher, Arnold Toynbee) are both antimedia and pro-resurrection. At one time, Pittsburgh had a total of six of the tiles at busy intersections, making an "L" shape when the locations were pinpointed on a map. As for how they got there, it is believed that during the 1980s and 1990s, the tiles were dropped at a few intersections and pushed into the road by car tires passing over top. Today, none of the original Toynbee tiles remain visible in the streets, but a copycat

TOYNBEE TILES

WHAT Tiles with odd phrases left in the middle of Pittsburgh intersections

WHERE Forbes and Ross Streets

COST Free to view

PRO TIP Please be safe when checking out the tiles and watch out for traffic.

www.toynbeeidea.com/portfolio/where/

Toynbee Tiles have been found in roughly two dozen cities in the United States.

While no original Toynbee Tiles are still embedded into Pittsburgh's streets, you can still see House of Hades tiles, similar in style and theme. Photo credit: Steven Locke

version, House of Hades tiles, can be seen at busy intersections along Boulevard of the Allies.

Over the years, additional tiles have been found all over the United States and in South America. People have tried to decipher the words, and theories abound, but there's one thing for sure: the tiles mention resurrection on planet Jupiter.

PANCAKES FIT FOR A PRESIDENT

Where can you get a plate of pancakes favored by a recent President?

When US President Barack Obama (then, Senator Obama) visited Pittsburgh in 2008 during his first presidential campaign, he hit the Strip District for breakfast one morning with some staff and really took a liking to the crepe-style pancakes at Pamela's Diner. Of course, local and national media surrounded the visit, curious for answers to pertinent news questions and how his campaign was going. To the surprise of the press, the first words to come out of his mouth were about the pancakes, giving positive publicity to the already-well-known-by-Pittsburghers restaurant.

If you've never been to Pamela's, you are truly missing out on one of the best breakfast foods in Pittsburgh. Thin with crispy edges, the crepe pancakes are a huge draw, and lines of patrons waiting for a seat stretch around the corner of the restaurant's exterior, especially on weekends. While either syrup or strawberries and cream are popular toppings, Obama preferred them plain.

And he didn't forget about them after the election, either: owners Gail Klingensmith and Pam Cohen were invited to the White House for a Memorial Day breakfast with war veterans. President Obama was not able to return to Pamela's during his two terms in office, but the First Lady Michelle Obama did make the trip.

The owners of Pamela's Diner have actually visited the White House twice.

President Obama loved Pamela's Diner and its famous crepe-style pancakes.
Photo credit: Steven Locke

P&G'S PAMELA'S DINER

WHAT President Obama's adoration for the thin, crepe-style breakfast food

WHERE 60 21st St.

COST Menu prices vary

PRO TIP Pamela's gets super busy, especially for breakfast on weekends, so it's best to queue up early.

www.pamelasdiner.com

A SPACESHIP BUILT FOR KIDS

Where can you test-drive toys inside a building built like a spaceship?

Ever wanted to hang out inside a spaceship and pretend you're a kid again? Or maybe you simply have young children and are looking for a spot to test-drive some toys before you take them home, so they won't end up buried at the bottom of a toy box. No matter what the reason, Playthings Etc. in Butler is where you need to head. Just a few miles north of Pittsburgh proper, you can do both.

Dubbing itself the "World's Coolest Toy Store," one trip to the parking lot explains why. The giant spaceship there looks like it's ready for takeoff as it sits on a raised center line. And, if you like sentimental detail tie-ins, its interior Space Portal stars are accurately positioned to indicate their bearings at the store's latitude and longitude on December 30th—the date the owners were married. Its front doors are massive and make for for a fun photo opp too.

Sure, the shiny aluminum, welded exterior is a definite draw, but the coolest part about the store is walking through the massive front doors and being encouraged to try out almost any toy in the place. You can take a spin on a scooter, try on a few kooky masks, camp out in a small circus tent for a few minutes, or play a card game with one of the shopkeepers.

PLAYTHINGS ETC.

WHAT A toy store built like a spaceship

WHERE 2483 William Flynn Hwy., Butler, PA 16001

COST Free to browse and test-drive toys

PRO TIP If you have kids, you'll definitely want to carve out a couple of hours to browse and play.

www.playthings-etc.com

Walk through the spaceship-style building's doors, and there are thousands of toys to buy and test-drive. Photo credit: Karyn Locke

This year, an outdoor scavenger hunt, created by the owners, offers fans a chance at collecting, and spending, free store gift cards. With puzzles and clues posted on its Facebook page, it's a first-solve, first-grab type of situation for the first few days of July. All the treasures are hidden within a 16-mile radius of the shop, which encourages folks to use their brains and knowledge of local landmarks.

Playthings Etc. has a stock of more than 6,000 toys.

CEMETERY FOR THE LIVING DEAD

Where can you go to recreate a famous horror movie scene?

On October 1, 1968, filmmaker George Romero officially started a new zombie trend: he was the first to give the undead free will, apart from a lust for human flesh, as opposed to being commanded by voodoo. The cult horror classic, *Night of the Living Dead,* was filmed around the Pittsburgh area for a mere $114,000 and grossed more than 250 times its budget at the box offices. For the movie's 50th anniversary in 2018, fans and the original cast all came together at the movie's first screening location, the Byham Theater in the Cultural District, to hear tales about filming on location in areas around the city.

But for all of its cult classic glory, the opening scene is probably its most famous. Filmed in Evans City Cemetery on Franklin Road, it stars siblings Johnny and Barbara as they visit their father's grave, only to be attacked by zombies. As for the film's most-famous line, "They're coming to get you, Barbara," it was spoken at the cemetery as well.

For visitors who want more than photos featuring both the Blair and Nicholas Kramer gravestones near where Barbara stood (and crouched!), there's a *Night of the Living Dead* Museum in Evans City filled with movie props and film memorabilia, plus some interactive experiences to keep the zombie love alive—or at least, undead.

EVANS CITY CEMETERY

WHAT *Night of the Living Dead* headstones

WHERE 8044 Franklin Road, Evans City, PA 16033

COST Free

PRO TIP The Blair headstone is pretty simple to find. As for the Kramer stone, once you pass the chapel on the left, it's about 325 meters farther on the right side.

Recreating the famous opening scene from Night of the Living Dead *at Evans City Cemetery. Photo credit: Steven Locke*

Night of the Living Dead has grossed $30 million total since its debut in 1968.

KITCHEN TOWEL TURNED RALLY ICON

How did an old kitchen towel turn into an iconic rally item?

In Pittsburgh, if you're a Steelers fan, you never have to worry about standing alone in your fandom. Heinz Field home games are frequently sold out, and Steelers Nation fans pride themselves on filling the stadium while covering themselves from head to toe in black and gold and waving the famous gold-colored rally icon, the "Terrible Towel." Fans twirl their towels around in the air for touchdowns, turnovers, increased emotion, and just about any other reason to show their Steelers pride at the field, at bars, and at home in front of their televisions.

But the brightly hued dish-dryer towel wasn't invented by a housewife with a flair for 1970s earth tones; instead, it came from Pittsburgh Steelers' game announcer, Myron Cope. Trying to unite fans during a 1975 playoff game, he asked them to take bright yellow kitchen towels to the games and wave them in the air to show support.

TERRIBLE TOWEL

WHAT The rally icon of Pittsburgh Steelers' fans

WHERE At Heinz Field and in the homes of Steelers' fans

COST Prices vary, but roughly $10

PRO TIP Head to the Strip District for the best prices or look online if you're not in the city.

The first official Terrible Towels were sold for $6 in 1978.

A must-have Pittsburgh rally icon if you're a Steelers fan: a Terrible Towel. Photo credit: Karyn Locke

The idea soared like a Terry Bradshaw pass, and by Superbowl X in 1976, Myron Cope's bright gold Terrible Towels were circling like lassos in the hands of fans who watched their team win against the Dallas Cowboys. Mr. Cope gave the monetary rights to Allegheny Valley School in 1996 and proceeds have given $1.1 million to the school so far.

DON'T GO IN THE BASEMENT!

Where can you get the pants scared off you around Halloween?

Every horror movie lover knows never to go into the basement at a creepy house, especially when it's haunted. Remember the days of funhouse-style haunted houses filled with jump scares and dark lighting where the spooks in the basement were just employees dressed up in gruesome Halloween costumes? A lot has changed since those days, particularly in the Strip District. The Scarehouse, Pittsburgh's top-rated haunted house (and the Scariest Haunted House in America according to ABC News), offers an extreme version of its already super-scary haunts in a separate area called the Basement that's not for folks who are even close to timid.

After signing a release waiver (yes, it's that intense), willing guests are subjected to extreme conditions including tight spaces, loud screams, complete darkness, water, violent scenarios, and being left alone to contemplate their fear. Add in some pungent scents and profanity and it's a creepy cocktail that has some folks crying to leave or crying from happiness because they survived the psychological torture.

Each R-rated experience lasts about 45 minutes, but folks who have visited claim that the time in the Basement feels like it goes much slower. And, while a visit may sound like a complete nightmare for many, it sells out each Halloween season to both solo visitors and couples.

The Scarehouse had several paranormal investigations by the Ghost Hunters team at its previous location.

THE SCAREHOUSE

Love getting truly scared? A visit to the Basement at the Scarehouse is just what you need. Photo credit: www.flickr.com/photos/scarehousescott/

THE SCAREHOUSE

WHAT Top-rated haunted house with multiple themes and an even creepier basement

WHERE 2420 Penn Ave.

COST Prices vary depending on time of year and night

PRO TIP The Scarehouse is super popular, especially right before Halloween. It's best to lock down your tickets online before you visit.

www.scarehouse.com

IT'S A BIRD! IT'S A PLANE! IT'S . . . AN ACORN?

Where can you see remnants of an item from space that's not supposed to exist?

The bizarre tale of the Kecksburg Space Acorn reads like something out of an old sci-fi comic book. Across the sky of Canada and North America on December 5, 1965, a fireball wailed through the darkness over the small town of Kecksburg, Pennsylvania after causing small fires in Ohio and Pennsylvania as its blazing debris fell from the sky before it eventually landed. Both adults and children saw it; a few ran to see where it landed, and curiosity was piqued.

But here's where the story offers several possible outcomes: Kecksburg witnesses claim it landed in the nearby woods and looked like a 10-foot-long acorn (roughly the size of a small car), complete with hieroglyphic writing around its base. When the Army finally arrived, they posted armed guards near the supposed sight where it landed and turned away the curious townsfolk looking for validation, only to later state that there was nothing found. The next day, an official statement was released blaming a meteor crash on the midnight chaos.

In 1990, *Unsolved Mysteries* came to town to feature the still-debated event in one of its episodes. The show's investigators recreated the alleged UFO and its backstory

KECKSBURG SPACE ACORN

WHAT A left-behind prop piece from Unsolved Mysteries

WHERE 5113 Water St., Mt. Pleasant

COST Free

PRO TIP If you're really into aliens and UFOs, the city's annual festival will be right up your street!

https://kecksburgvfd.com/ufo-festival-events/

The lifesize Kecksburg Space Acorn, high atop a platform for visitors to see. Photo credit: Steven Locke

from firsthand sketches and witness recollections, and the life-size Kecksburg Space Acorn was born. After the filming, the crew left the giant prop behind, so citizens put it on a platform on a prominent hillside hoping to draw attention to the town. To add to the fun, Kecksburg hosts its annual UFO Festival each summer.

Kecksburg's annual UFO Festival has a Bed Race where participants decorate and push beds on wheels. Winners receive money and a plaque.

I THOUGHT MARS WAS 172 MILLION MILES AWAY...

Where can you visit a quaint city named after a planet?

Space aliens. NASA scientists. Astronomists. Butler County, Pennsylvania. What do these four things have in common? A love of the planet Mars, of course! All comparisons aside, there'd be no Martians to ramp up our science fiction stories without the fourth planet from the Sun. Scientists have made more interplanetary visits to Mars (via orbitors and rovers) than to any other heavenly body in the solar system, and the small borough of Mars, Pennsylvania, is all about it. In fact, the community hosts a Mars Exploration Celebration Days event annually. Annual for planet Mars, that is. The Mars lunar year is 687 Earth days, so it falls roughly every two years for us non-Martians.

The local weekend festival draws in more than just Mars and Pittsburgh residents: NASA scientists showcase what's new and innovative regarding planetary exploration, and they offer

MARS EXPLORATION CELEBRATION DAYS

WHAT A festival giving tribute to the planet Mars

WHERE Pittsburgh St. and Crowe Ave., Mars

COST Free

PRO TIP Celebration Days are very family-friendly, so feel free to take the kids!

www.visitbutlercounty.com/events/33311-m/mars-exploration-celebration-days

Last year's Exploration Celebration had a free Escape Room created by local high school students.

A trip to Mars is only a few miles north of Pittsburgh! Photo credit: Molly Ramirez

a heavy focus on STEAM (science, technology, engineering, arts, and mathematics) activities to get kids involved in the fun. And to add to the spacey ambiance, a permanent Martian UFO sculpture is parked on the corner of Pittsburgh Street and Grand Avenue.

The tribute to Mars is anything but hokey and includes live performances, exhibits, and local vendors, as well as a Blast-Off Dinner and a NASA scientist meet and greet to officially kick off the Martian new year.

BURIED TO HIS CAR

Why was a Corvette turned into a final resting place and buried in the ground?

When George E. Swanson bought his wife a white 1984 Corvette, it was he who fell in love with it instead of the other way around. In fact, Swanson was so enamored of the car that he vowed to make it his final resting place. On May 25, 1994, Swanson was buried with his car.

To make his final wish come true, Mr. Swanson purchased 12 adjacent burial plots at Brush Creek Cemetery in Irwin, and, after much debate between him and the cemetery owners, they agreed to let him be buried in his sports car. So, when he passed away in March of 1994, his wife had his body cremated and kept the ashes in an urn until the private service could be held.

In fulfillment of his wishes, his urn was placed in the driver's seat along with a handmade quilt from the ladies of his church, and his favorite song, "Release Me" by Engelbert Humperdink, was queued up and ready to play on the car's cassette deck at the service. To add to the sentimentality, a note from his wife was lovingly added inside the car. And just so visitors to the location and passersby would know about his passion for the 'vette, Mrs. Swanson had a likeness of his beloved vehicle carved onto his headstone.

GEORGE E. SWANSON GRAVE

WHAT A Corvette buried in the ground along with its owner

WHERE Brush Creek Cemetery, 127 Altar Ln., Irwin

COST Free to view

PRO TIP Head left after the cemetery's main gate, and stay on the main road. You'll need to keep an eye out for the carved corvette on his headstone.

www.findagrave.com/memorial/14001374/george-e_-swanson

George E. Swanson, the man who loved his wife's Corvette so much he was buried in it.
Photo credit: Steven Locke

Swanson's Corvette was drained of its fluids for environmental protection before being buried.

WELCOME TO THE FIVE-STAR JUNGLE

Where can you visit a five-star animal refuge near Pittsburgh?

When you drive up to the front entrance to Nemacolin Woodlands Resort's Chateau Lafayette in the Laurel Highlands, you can't help but notice the 19th-century European architecture, its pristine landscaping, the large art pieces around it, and its similarities to the luxurious Ritz Paris in France. But, keep cruising along to the rear of the resort's vast acreage, and you'll spy a small airport, an art museum, and a wildlife refuge in keeping with the five-star surroundings.

Both domestic and exotic animals are cared for on the property, and they include larger animals such as lions, tigers, wolves, and red sheep. Head to the Animal Ambassador building, and you'll find smaller—but still just as beautiful—animals, including reptiles, a striped skunk, and a kinkajou. While the giant cats are undoubtedly the most impressive animals, Billy Goat Mountain will give you the most laughs as the funny, hooved creatures are always getting into something or trying to knock each other off.

Nemacolin's owner, Maggie Hardy, attributes the Wildlife Academy and animal refuge to her father's love of animals and a willingness to rescue many of its inhabitants from failing zoos or poor conditions. With heavy safety measures put in place, resort

---

A fun time to visit is during baby animal season in the spring. If you're adamant about seeing the little cuties, feel free to call and ask about the resort's new additions.

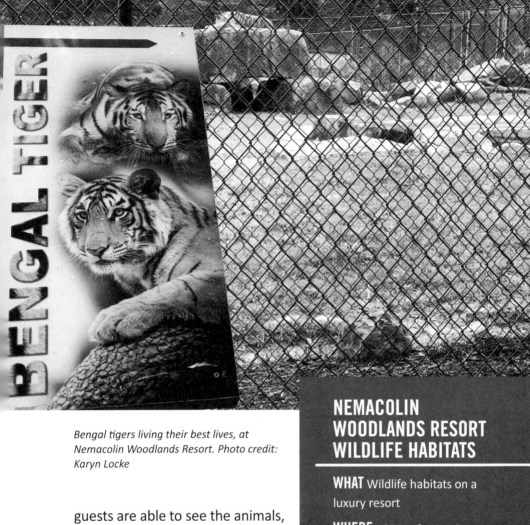

Bengal tigers living their best lives, at Nemacolin Woodlands Resort. Photo credit: Karyn Locke

guests are able to see the animals, feed a few on one of its tours, and learn about conservation while enjoying the view.

NEMACOLIN WOODLANDS RESORT WILDLIFE HABITATS

WHAT Wildlife habitats on a luxury resort

WHERE 1001 Lafayette Dr., Farmington

COST Free

PRO TIP You can walk around and see the animals for free, but a tour is the way to go, especially if you want to learn more about the refuge and its inhabitants.

www.nemacolin.com/activities/wildlife

AL, OH, AND MO!

Where can you see three sky-high fish?

Do you have someone in your family who has an "I almost caught a fish THIS big" story or a friend who talks about the fish that he was close to catching until it escaped the fishing rod at the last minute?

Outside the Children's Museum Pittsburgh, there are three massive fishy friends who, as their story goes, are on the other side of the tale of the ones that got away. As this story goes, there is one from each of the Pittsburgh rivers making for whimsical delight for both children and adults, particularly on windy days when they turn in the wind like weather vanes. And as we always love a good happy ending, these are the three who lived to tell their tale.

Officially titled *Al, Mo, and Oh: The Three That Got Away*, you'll spy these three larger-than-life bass fish on poles in the museum parking lot. And when I say larger, I mean larger: each 14-foot long fish is made from fiberglass and weighs roughly 400 pounds! The three have unique, individual painting schemes, and their large, closed mouths aren't saying any more about it.

AL, OH, AND MO

WHAT Larger than life bass art pieces

WHERE Children's Museum Pittsburgh, 10 Children's Way

COST Art is free to view but, if you want to visit the museum: Adults $16, Children 2–18 $14, Seniors 60+ $14, Children under 2 Free

PRO TIP Purchase your tickets online for a discounted rate.

https://pittsburghkids.org

Children's Museum Pittsburgh opened in 1983 in the former Allegheny Post Office on the North Side.

Al, Oh, and Mo, *the three bass that whirl and spin at Children's Museum Pittsburgh.*
Photo credit: Steven Locke

The aquatic trio made its debut on July 25, 2005. Named for the first syllable of each of the three prominent Pittsburgh waterways (Allegheny, Monongahela, and Ohio Rivers), the public art piece was created by Elizabeth and Chris Seifert.

NERDY GARDEN

Where can you visit a garden fashioned after a drawing template?

If numerical sequencing and beautiful, curved lines hold your interest, you're undoubtedly happy to call yourself a math nerd in the most positive way. And if you were to step onto the roof of the Posner Center at Carnegie Mellon University in Oakland, you'd be among both art lovers and garden enthusiasts, as well as CMU students who share a love of sculpture for math-passionate people.

Located at the Kraus Campo, the garden was designed and created by alumnus Mel Bochner and landscape artist Michael Van Valkenburgh. Its inspiration came all the way from Greece, believe it or not. Wanting an agora-type setting where students could gather to listen to teachers discuss philosophy and in turn start their own conversations, the garden is designed to encourage some deep, constructive thinking. The Green Roof was dedicated in 2004 and has fulfilled its mission as a peaceful spot ever since.

THE KRAUS CAMPO

WHAT A sculpture shaped like a French curve surrounded by a pristine garden setting

WHERE Carnegie Mellon University

COST Free

PRO TIP The Kraus Campo is on the Posner Center's Green Roof between the College of Fine Arts building and the Tepper School of Business.

www.cmu.edu/cmtoday/issues/august-2005-issue/feature-stories/the-kraus-campo

But the real star of the landscape show is the *Campo* at the garden center. With dimensions of 25 by 60 by 3 feet in height, the sculpture is shaped like a French curve (a drafting template used for manually drawing curved lines) and flows beautifully with black-and-white numerical tiles that highlight the numerical sequencing found in curving lines, all the while surrounded by blooming plants and shrubbery.

French curve botanical beauty. Photo credit: Steven Locke

The Kraus Campo has a 58-foot-long tiled quote that reads backwards.

EXTINCT ATTACK

Where can you see a taxidermy piece with actual human bones?

Walking through the large rooms and along the wide floors of Carnegie Museum of Natural History as a child, a particular exhibit always stood out to me; it turns out, I wasn't alone in my fascination. Not your typical mid-19th century taxidermy diorama, *Lion Attacking a Dromedary* depicts a lion attacking a man atop a camel. The details have always been hauntingly real, stopping viewers in their tracks for a closer look. But in 2018, the popular Pittsburgh museum found out there was much more to the piece than originally thought.

Acquired in 1898 from the American Museum of Natural History in New York City for fifty dollars, a CT scan was performed on the piece during routine restoration work before moving it to a new location in the museum. Not only did the piece get refreshed, it was discovered that the camel rider's head was actually composed of a real human skull—including its teeth.

Previously thinking the exact opposite, the museum put the piece back on display and concerned themselves with what to do next. Considerations included returning the human

LION ATTACKING A DROMEDARY TAXIDERMY

WHAT A taxidermy piece with real human bones and teeth

WHERE 4400 Forbes Ave.

COST Museum admission: Adults $19.95, Seniors 65+ $14.95, Students with ID $11.95, Children 3-18 $11.95

PRO TIP Look for the piece near the Grand Staircase.

carnegiemnh.org

Taxidermy was started in England during the early 1800s.

More than just a 19th-century taxidermy piece. Photo credit: www.flickr.com/photos/benledbetter-architect

skull back to its original place to be buried, but DNA testing would probably not prove where it came from. Happily, continued research is being done to try to narrow it down.

Originally titled *Arab Courier Attacked by Lions*, the exhibit piece not only includes human remains but also has actual taxidermy Barbary lions, according to its records. DNA samples have been taken in an attempt to prove the species and, if found to be accurate, will showcase not only human bones but the bodies of now-extinct lions that were once found in North Africa.

STEEL TO STEELERS LOGO

How did a popular city logo turn into an NFL team's icon?

Think about the most successful NFL teams in our country, and the Pittsburgh Steelers are at the top of the list—and not just for the number of fans they have. As titles go, they're tied with the New England Patriots for having won six Super Bowls each. But have you ever looked at a Steelers' helmet and considered how the team's famous logo came about? It's all due to a love of the steel industry.

In 1962, Steelers' owner Art Rooney based the team's logo on the US Steel Corporation's Steelmark logo. In order to use the three hypocycloids (squares with inward-curving lines) in yellow, orange, and blue (for coal, iron ore, and scrap, respectively), Rooney had to petition the American Iron and Steel Institute to change the "Steel" to "Steelers." Once the go-ahead was given, the color tones were changed to fit the team, so the yellow became gold, the orange became red, and the bright blue was made darker.

Upon receiving the approval, Rooney was still not sure that the new logo was a good one, so

PITTSBURGH STEELERS' LOGO

WHAT How US Steel's logo turned into the famous football team's logo

WHERE On players' helmets and fan memorabilia

COST Free to admire

PRO TIP A true Steelers fan? Look in the city or online for a few souvenirs, and then impress your friends with your new logo-origin knowledge.

The Pittsburgh Steelers have won six Super Bowl Championships to date, four between 1975 and 1980.

The famous US Steel turned Pittsburgh Steelers logo on a flag in the Strip District. Photo credit: Steven Locke

he asked equipment manager Jack Hart to put it only on the right side of the gold helmets. Fortunately, the logo was a hit along with its one-sided placement, and both were kept as is. To this day, the Pittsburgh Steelers are the only team to display the team logo on only one side of its helmets.

SOURCES

Steeped in Danger: Miaschi, John. "Steepest Streets in the World." World Atlas, Jul. 16, 2019. www.worldatlas.com/articles/steepest-streets-in-the-world.html.

1+1=1?: "Confluence - Three Rivers (Pittsburgh, Pennsylvania) | Water, Geography." Wikimapia. https://wikimapia.org/1198433/Confluence-Three-Rivers.

AllOhMon or Aztec Gold?: Potter, Chris. "Why Are the Bridges in Pittsburgh Painted Yellow?" *Pittsburgh City* paper, December 4, 2003. www.pghcitypaper. com/pittsburgh/why-are-the-bridges-in-pittsburgh-painted-yellow/Content?oid=1335862.

The Most Heavily Painted Object in the World: "Carnegie Mellon University School Spirit Traditions." Carnegie Mellon University. https://admission.enrollment.cmu.edu/pages/carnegie-mellon-school-spirit-traditions .

Houdini Jumped the Bridge: Sebak, Rick. "Harry Houdini's Handcuffed Pittsburgh Plunges." *Pittsburgh* magazine, Feb. 19, 2005. www. pittsburghmagazine.com/harry-houdinis-handcuffed-pittsburgh-plunges/.

Emoticon-ing Our Feelings: "Happy 25th, Emoticon." www.cmu.edu/homepage/beyond/2007/summer/happy-25th-emoticon.shtml.

Wood You Care to Drive?: Krauss, Margaret J. "The Surprising Story of Pittsburgh's Last Wooden Street." *Pittsburgh* magazine, September 28, 2015. www.pittsburghmagazine.com/the-surprising-story-of-pittsburghs-last-wooden-street/.

Where the Streets Have No Pave: "South Side Steps," http://secretpittsburgh.pitt.edu/location/250.

Don't Run Over My Chair!: Slaby, M. J. "The Pittsburgh Parking Chair's History, Mystery, and Rules." Incline, December 17, 2018. https://archive.theincline.com/2018/12/17/the-pittsburgh-parking-chairs-history-mystery-and-rules/.

I'm Inclined to Go to Work: Natalie, J. "How to Ride the Pittsburgh Inclines." Pittsburgh. www.visitpittsburgh.com/blog/how-to-ride-the-pittsburgh-inclines/.

A Silent Night—Interrupted by Radio: "KDKA Begins to Broadcast 1920." PBS. www.visitpittsburgh.com/blog/how-to-ride-the-pittsburgh-inclines/.

Wheels in His Head: "Ferris Wheel Inventor Historical Marker." Explore PA History. https://explorepahistory.com/hmarker. php?markerId=1-A-35D.

You Want a Map with That?: "Pittsburgh Was the Home of the Country's First Gas Station." The Almanac. November 29, 2013. https://thealmanac. net/archives/pittsburgh-was-the-home-of-the-country-s-first-gas/article_40497252-d9cc-53de-a20c-cfa6076093c6.html.

Play Ball!: "Forbes Field." Ball Parks of Baseball. www. ballparksofbaseball.com/ ballparks/forbes-field/.

Let's Have Some Make-Believe: "Mister Rogers' Neighborhood." Heinz History Center. www.heinzhistorycenter.org/exhibits/mister-rogers-neighborhood.

Come on In, the Door's Open; "What Is Doors Open?" https://doorsopenpgh.org.

Stop Downtown, Get a Free "T:" "Fare Free Public Transport Pittsburgh, PAPA," https://freepublictransport.info/city/pittsburgh/.

Waterlogged: "About Kennywood,"www.kennywood.com/about-kennywood; "Garfield's Nightmare," www.kennywood.com/Garfields-nightmare.

The Plush Life: "About Anthrocon," www.anthrocon.org/about.

Dead Men Walking: Pittsburgh Zombie Fest, www. pittsburghzombiefest.com; the Monroeville Mall World record Attempt Zombie Walk, www.theitsaliveshow.com/ZombieWalkMonroevilleMall.htm.

Not Just Natural, *Post*Natural: www.postnatural.org.

The Best View in the House, er, City: "The 10 Most Beautiful Places in America." *USA Today*. September 30, 2013. www. usatoday. com/story/life/weekend/2013/09/30/the-10-most-beautiful-places-in-america/2754657/.

A Garden of Biblical Proportions: "The Largest Biblical Garden in North America." Rodef Shalom. www.rodefshalombiblicalgarden. org/garden-history/.

Won't You Be My North Shore Neighbor?: Mavrogianis, Alex. "Nine Things You May Not Know about the Mister Rogers Statue." *Pittsburgh* magazine. Sep. 4, 2016. www.pittsburghmagazine. com/9-things-you-may-not-know-about-the-mister-rogers-statue/.

Speak Slow and Easy around the Omni William Penn Hotel: "Speakeasy Downtown Pittsburgh." Omni Hotels & Resorts. www. omnihotels.com/ hotels/pittsburgh-william-penn/dining/the-speakeasy; "Whiskey Rebellion." Encyclopaedia Britannica. www. britannica.com/event/Whiskey- Rebellion.

Buried to Their Jobs: Glaser, Arthur E. "History of Allegheny Observatory." University of Pittsburgh. Updated May 25, 2001. www.pitt.edu/~aobsvtry/history_frame.html.

Underwater Submersible in the Ohio: "History of the USS Requin (SS 481)." Carnegie Science Center. www.carnegiesciencecenter. org/exhibits/requin-submarine-history.

Wait a 35-Foot Minute!: "Pittsburgh's Coca-Cola Clock." The Brookline Connection. www. brooklineconnection.com/history/ Facts/CocaColaClock.html.

Unusual "Manor"isms: www.trundlemanor.com.

Mad for Music Boxes: Bayernhof Museum, www. bayernhofmuseum.com/index.html.

The Ginch Who Collects Musical Memorabilia: Johnny Angel's Ginchy Stuff, www.jaginchystuff.com.

Randy with Art: Randyland, https://randyland.com.

Second to the Vatican: Wilkinson, Rachel. "A Pittsburgh Church Holds the Greatest Collection of Relics Outside of the Vatican." *Smithsonian* magazine. July 2017. www.smithsonianmag.com/ arts-culture/pittsburgh-church-greatest-collection-relics-outside-vatican-180963680.

You Look Smashing, Atom: Eschner, Kat. "The Strange Story of the Westinghouse Atom Smasher." *Smithsonian* magazine. December 20, 2016. www.smithsonianmag.com/smart-news/strange-story-westinghouse-atom-smasher-180961515/.

Pittsburgh's Dippy Patron Sponsors Dino: "Hip Dinosaur Dippy, Oakland's Trendy Dinosaur." *Pittsburgh Post-Gazette*. June 25, 2014. https://newsinteractive.post-gazette.com/ thedigs/2014/06/25/hip-dinosaur-dippy-oaklands-trendy-dinosaur/; "Discovering Dippy."Carnegie Museum of Natural History. carnegiemnh.org/discovering-dippy.

Man of Steel: Misko, Stephanie. "Pennsylvania Folklore... or Is It Fakelore?" Pennsylvania Center for the Book. Fall 2008. http://pabook2.libraries.psu.edu/palitmap/ JoeMagarac.html.

Emerald Ring around the Neighbors: Emerald View Park, https://mwcdc.org/park/; "Emerald View Park." Landforce. www.landforcepgh.org/hire-landforce/past-projects/emerald-view-park.

Murals to the Max(o): The Murals of Maxo Vanka, https://vankamurals.org/general-info.

This Zoo's for the Birds: "About Us." National Aviary. www.aviary.org/about-us.

A Jaw-Dropping Front Door: "Thoughts on the Fort Pitt Tunnel." *Pittsburgh Post Gazette*. August 28, 2014. www.post-gazette.com/local/south/2014/08/28/Yelp-thoughts-Fort-Pitt- Tunnel-Pittsburgh/stories/201408280022.

In-House Publications: "History| City of Asylum." City of Asylum. https://cityofasylum.org/about/history.

Invention Incubation: "An Immersive Environment to Spark Your Creativity." InventionLand. https://inventionland.com.

Rust Belt Beauty: "Arts & Grounds Tour." Rivers of Steel. www.riversofsteel.com/experiences/tours/arts-grounds-tour.

24/7 "Soup"er Cemetery: "Andy Warhol's Grave." Andy Warhol Museum. www.warhol.org/andy-warhols-life/ figment.

A Light Display to Make Clark Griswold Green with Envy: Klein, Hal B. "Every Night Is Light-Up Night at Bob's Garage in Blawnox." *Pittsburgh City Paper*. December 11, 2013. www.pghcitypaper.com/pittsburgh/ every-night-is-light-up-night-at-bobs-garage-in-blawnox/ Content?oid=1715533.

You Put What on That Sandwich?: "Our Story." "Primanti Bros. https://primantibros.com/story.

Best Cake in America: Parrish, Marlene. "A Taste of Pittsburgh: Burnt Almond Torte." *Pittsburgh Post-Gazette*. March 18, 2015. www.post-gazette.com/life/food/2015/03/18/A-taste-of-Pittsburgh-Burnt-Almond-Torte/stories/201503110004.

Mostly Cloudy with a Chance of More Clouds: Misachi, John. "The Cloudiest Cities in the United States." World Atlas. www.worldatlas.com/articles/the-cloudiest-cities-in-the-united-states.html; "Cloudiest Cities in The United States Top 10." Legit Informant. January 3, 2020. https://legitinformant.com/cloudiest-cities-in-the-united-states-top-10.

Heaven, I'm in (Bicycle) Heaven: "About Us." Bicycle Heaven. www.bicycleheaven.org/pages/about-us.

Catsup to Pittsburgh: Napsha, Joe. "The Company Ketchup Built: Heinz, Started in Pittsburgh, Celebrates 150 Years." The Morning Call. October 14, 2019. www.mcall.com/business/mc-biz-heinz-ketchup-celebrates-anniversary-20191014-ya6emsoehbg7leruvp6kxtkowa-story.html.

31 Cultural Celebrations Under One Roof: "Nationality Rooms | About." University of Pittsburgh. www.nationalityrooms.pitt.edu/about.

The Best 360-Degree View of the City—But Only Once a Year: "BLAST! at Comcast Light-Up Night." Pittsburgh Downtown Partnership. https://downtownpittsburghholidays.com/blast.

Pickled Tink: "Picklesburgh Has Deep Pickle Roots." www.picklesburgh.com/about-picklesburgh.

Deconsecrated Brew: The Church Brew Works, https://churchbrew.com.

Old-School Oysters: "Our Story." The Original Oyster House. www.originaloysterhousepittsburgh.com/our-story.

Pittsburghese: "Pittsburghese Overview." University of Pittsburgh. http://pittsburghspeech.pitt.edu/PittsburghSpeech_PgheseOverview.html; "Pittsburgh Speech and Society." University of Pittsburgh. http://pittsburghspeech.pitt.edu/PittsburghSpeech_History.html.

Beer City?: Clark, Jane. "Where the Bars Are: Top US Cities for Drinkers." *USA Today*. December 6, 2013. www.usatoday.com/story/dispatches/2013/12/06/top-bar-and-pizza-cities/3882089/.

20 Years of "H"Contention: "The Pittsburgh H." Visit Pittsburgh. www.visitpittsburgh.com/things-to-do/arts-culture/history/the-pittsburgh-h/.

Defy Gravity in North Park: Danner, Christi. "This Unnerving Phenomenon in a Pennsylvania Town Is Too Weird for Words." Only in Your State. January 25, 2016. www.onlyinyourstate.com/pennsylvania/pa-gravity-hill/.

Go Steagles!: Readmikenow. "Steagles: The 1943 Combination of the Steelers and Eagles." How They Play. March 26, 2019. https://howtheyplay.com/team-sports/STEAGLES-The-1943-NFL-Team-that-combined-players-from-the-Pittsburgh-Steelers-and-Philadelphia-Eagles.

Immaculate Domination: Associated Press. "Immaculate Reception Honored." ESPN. December 22, 2012. www.espn.com/nfl/story/_/id/8773581/pittsburgh-steelers-unveil-immaculate-reception-monument.

Seldom-Seen Beauty: Jones, Diana Nelson. "Walkabout: Seldom Seen a Treasure Hidden in City." *Post-Gazette*. July 15, 1999. https://old.post-gazette.com/columnists/19990715walk.asp.

Tunnels of Fun Facts: Blackley, Katie. "Over the River and through the Hills: Everything You Never Knew about Pittsburgh's Iconic Tunnels." WESA. August 9, 2017. www.wesa.fm/post/over-river-and-through-hills-everything-you-never-knew-about-pittsburghs-iconic-tunnels#stream/0.

Where Trolleys Go to Die: Bundy, Jared. "Stranger Things in the Laurel Highlands."Laurel Highlands, Pennsylvania. Oct, 27, 2017. www.laurelhighlands.org/blog/post/stranger-things-in-the-laurel-highlands.

Do You Want Three Scoops or Four?: Subranamiam, Arthi. "Banana Split Is Turning 115 and There's a Festival to Celebrate It." Post-Gazette. August 21, 2019. www.post-gazette.com/life/food/2019/08/21/Banana-split-turns-115-years-old-in-Latrobe/stories/201908210077.

Don't Throw Out My Stuff!: "The Warhol: Art, Film and Video, Archives." www.warhol.org/art-and-archives.

East of Tinseltown: "Pittsburgh: 'Hollywood East.'" www. pghfilm. org/4298-2.

"Ladies and Gentlemen, I Give You . . . the Sky!": "Pittsburgh Trivia." Pittsburgh. www.visitpittsburgh.com/about-us/about-pittsburgh/pittsburgh-trivia/ ; "Arena History." www.web. archive. org/web/20081208034146/www.mellonarena.com/site41.php.

Four-Season Miniature Fun: "The Miniature Railroad & Village® Celebrating 100 Years of Engineering Memories." Carnegie Science Center. www.carnegiesciencecenter.org/exhibits/miniature-railroad.

"Mist"erious Path: "Tales of the Blue Myst Road." www.weirdus. com/states/pennsylvania/roadside_oddities/blue_mist_road.

Public Art with Foresight: Lancianese, Adelina. "Look Down: How Toynbee Tiles Invaded (and Disappeared from) Pittsburgh Streets." WESA. June 12, 2018. www.wesa.fm/post/look-down-how-toynbee-tiles-invaded-and-disappeared-pittsburgh-streets#stream/0.

Pancakes Fit for a President: Carpenter, Mackenzie. "Obama Takes a Liking to Pamela's Pancakes." *Post-Gazette*. Apr. 22, 2008. www.post-gazette.com/news/early-returnsmenulink/2008/04/22/Obama-takes-a-liking-to-Pamela-s-pancakes/stories/200804220235.

A Spaceship Built for Kids: Locke, Karyn. "All the Fun Things to Do in Butler County." Sand or Snow. June 17, 2019. www.sandandorsnow.com/2019/06/fun-things-to-do-in-butler-county-pa.

Cemetery for the Living Dead: "The Living Dead Museum and Gift Shop." www.livingdeadmuseum.com/museum.html.

Kitchen Towel Turned Rally Icon: "The History of the Terrible Towel." Visit Pittsburgh. www.visitpittsburgh.com/things-to-do/pittsburgh-sports-teams/terrible-towel.

Don't Go in The Basement!: Scarehouse: Basement Ticket, www.scarehouse.com/haunts/the-basement/.

It's a Bird! It's a Plane! It's . . . an Acorn?: Majors, Dan. "Five Decades Later, the Kecksburg UFO is Identified (Probably)." *Post-Gazette*. December 6, 2015. www.post-gazette.com/news/science/2015/12/06/50-years-later-the-Kecksburg-Westmoreland-County-UFO-is-identified-probably/stories/201512060146.

I Thought Mars was 172 Million Miles Away . . .: Borough of Mars, www.marsnewyear.com/mars-borough.

Buried to His Car: "Pennsylvania Man Buried with his Beloved Corvette." History. July 28, 2019. www.history.com/this-day-in-history/pennsylvania-man-buried-with-his-beloved-corvette.

Welcome to the Five-Star Jungle: "Welcome to the Jungle." Nemacolin. Feb. 14, 2020. www.nemacolin.com/activities/wildlife.

Oh, Al, & Mo!: "Children's Museum Pittsburgh Annual Report." March 3, 2020. http://s3.amazonaws.com/cmop_production/downloads/130/AR2005-2006.pdf.

Nerdy Garden: Sloss, Eric. "The Kraus Campo." Carnegie Mellon University. August 1, 2005. www.cmu.edu/cmtoday/issues/august-2005-issue/feature-stories/the-kraus-campo.

Extinct Attack: Ross, Delaney. "150-Year-Old Diorama Surprises Scientists with Human Remains." *National Geographic*. January 29, 2017. www.nationalgeographic.com/news/2017/01/taxidermy-carnegie-museum-skull/#close.

Steelers Logo: Helmet RP New Wires. "The Story behind the Steel Logo on Steelers' Helmet." Reliable Planet. March 6, 2020. www.reliableplant.com/Read/15573/story-behind-steel-logo-on-steelers'-helmet.

INDEX